BREAKING
POINT

BREAKING

POINT

THE NEW BIG SHIFTS
PUTTING CANADA AT RISK

DARRELL BRICKER & JOHN IBBITSON

SIGNAL

McCLELLAND
& STEWART

Signal and colophon are registered trademarks of
Penguin Random House Canada Limited.

The authorized representative in the EU for product safety and compliance is Penguin Random House Ireland, Morrison Chambers, 32 Nassau Street, Dublin D02 YH68, Ireland, https://eu-contact.penguin.ie

Library and Archives Canada Cataloguing in Publication

Title: Breaking point : the new big shifts putting Canada at risk /
Darrell Bricker and John Ibbitson.
Names: Bricker, Darrell Jay, 1961- author. | Ibbitson, John, author.
Identifiers: Canadiana (print) 20250236265 | Canadiana (ebook) 2025023937X |
ISBN 9780771030345 (hardcover) | ISBN 9780771030352 (EPUB)
Subjects: LCSH: Canada—Politics and government—21st century. | LCSH:
Canada—Economic conditions—21st century. | LCSH: Canada—Social
conditions—21st century. | LCSH: Canada—Emigration and immigration—
Government policy. | LCSH: Regionalism—Canada.
Classification: LCC JL65 .B755 2025 | DDC 320.971—dc23

Cover design by Kate Sinclair
Typeset in Adobe Caslon Pro by Daniella Zanchetta
Printed in Canada

Signal, an imprint of McClelland & Stewart
Penguin Random House Canada
320 Front Street West, Suite 1400
Toronto, Ontario, M5V 3B6, Canada
penguinrandomhouse.ca

1   2   3   4   5   29   28   27   26   25

Penguin
Random House
Canada

To Nina and Emily. Without you, there is no me.
—D.B.

For Grant, always.
—J.I.

CONTENTS

PREFACE

They were at it to the very end. Dominic LeBlanc, the minister charged with rescuing Canada from President Donald Trump's tariff threats, spent hours at the home of Commerce Secretary Howard Lutnick, trying to work out a deal. Marc-André Blanchard, Prime Minister Mark Carney's chief of staff, flew down to D.C. In Washington, Ambassador Kirsten Hillman lobbied relentlessly on the phone and on Capitol Hill. None of it worked. On August 1, 2025, the United States added new tariffs to the ones Trump had already imposed.

The president said he was punishing Canada because of fentanyl crossing the border, which was a lie. He railed against Canadian restrictions on dairy imports. He condemned Carney for deciding to recognize Palestine as a state.

None of the excuses really mattered because these weren't really tariff negotiations. This was a shakedown. Nice little country you got there, Trump was telling Carney. Shame if something happened to it. Why don't you just become the fifty-first state?

Canada–U.S. relations have never been this bad. But believe it or not, Trump is not the biggest threat our country faces. Our own worst enemy is ourselves.

Carney achieved an astonishing come-from-behind win in the federal election of April 28, 2025, because millions of Canadians believed that the former bank governor was best equipped to deal with Donald Trump's tariffs and threats of annexation. But the prime minister's minority government confronts a country riven with division. To prove the point, two powerful political leaders presented the prime minister with irreconcilably conflicting ultimatums immediately after the vote.

"A large majority of Albertans are deeply frustrated that the same government that overtly attacked our provincial economy almost unabated for the past 10 years has been returned to government," wrote Premier Danielle Smith. Albertans "will no longer tolerate having our industries threatened and our resources landlocked by Ottawa."[1]

At the same time, Bloc Québécois leader Yves-François Blanchet laid down his own ultimatum for keeping Carney's minority government alive. "There's no future for oil and gas, at least in Quebec and probably everywhere," he declared. "And this has to be said and protected."[2]

Our country is facing threats from without and from within: from an American president and from regional and generational divides. Carney's task is to heal those divisions, even as Canada undergoes profound political and demographic change.

In *The Big Shift* (2013), we wrote about the decline of the Laurentian elite. The political, bureaucratic, academic, journalistic, business, and cultural leaders inhabiting Toronto, Montreal, Ottawa, and other communities of southern Ontario and Quebec had forged Confederation and governed the country ever since, we wrote, mostly through consensus and mostly through their political instrument, the Liberal Party, the "Natural Governing Party of Canada."

But those elites were on the descendant, we believed, eclipsed by the rising power and influence of Western Canada, and by the millions of new Canadians, mostly from developing countries in Asia and elsewhere, who filled the 905—the ring of suburban cities that surround Toronto, named after their first area code—along with the Lower Mainland outside Vancouver. Those immigrants were more economically and culturally conservative than many native-born, we observed. In concert with Western voters, they formed a new conservative coalition that could compete with the Laurentian Liberals. Eventually, we predicted, the progressive parties—some combination of the Liberals, NDP, and Greens—would coalesce into a centre-left alternative to the centre-right conservative coalition, bringing two-party politics to the federal level, as could already be found in the Prairie provinces, British Columbia, and parts of Atlantic Canada.

Then Justin Trudeau won a boxing match, the Liberal leadership, and ultimately the country in the election of 2015.

"An election expected to confirm the 'Big Shift'—the alignment of suburban immigrants in Ontario with the rising power of the Conservative West—has created a movement of its own," Andrew Cohen wrote in the *Ottawa Citizen*. "It's less a shift than a stampede. To the Liberals."[3]

But the Big Shift never went away. During Justin Trudeau's nine years in office, the West continued to grow in power and influence. And the suburban cities surrounding the downtowns are even more populated—bloated, some would say—than before. By the end of his third mandate, Trudeau was widely disliked or worse, with Pierre Poilievre's Conservatives more than 20 percentage points ahead in the polls. But then Trudeau stepped down and was replaced by Mark Carney, even as Trump threatened Canada with tariffs and annexation. Millions deserted the Conservatives, choosing Carney and the Liberals as the safest response to the American challenge.

But while the Liberals continue to dominate in suburban Central Canada and in parts of the Lower Mainland, much of the rest of the country is divided. The Conservatives continue to own the Prairies, British Columbia's interior, and rural Ontario, and in 2025 they nibbled at the peripheries of the 905 and the Lower Mainland. Separatist parties remain powerful provincially and federally in Quebec. The NDP was decimated federally in 2025, but, governing in Manitoba and British Columbia, it is still more coherent than the Liberals at the provincial level.

And even as older voters embraced the Liberal Party in the cause of national unity—and in the cause of preserving their property equity and investments—younger voters drifted toward the Conservatives, who promised them tax breaks and help buying their first home. Working-class voters who abandoned the NDP are now more aligned with Conservatives than with other parties. And on April 28, women were more likely to vote Liberal, while men were more likely to vote Conservative.

Donald Trump's annexationist threats are the political equivalent of the COVID-19 pandemic: an external emergency that generates at least an illusion of national unity. But the underlying strains in the country remain. Each region is estranged from the other; the dispossessed young feel estranged from their pampered, entitled elders. Canadians are divided by region, generation, gender, and class. And now the Americans have turned from allies into adversaries.

Canada is at the breaking point.

ONE

THE TRUDEAU EXPERIMENT

A Canadian prime minister has three main jobs: first, keep the economy moving; second, keep the country together; third, handle the Americans. Over the course of nine-plus years, Justin Trudeau failed at all of them.

Not completely, mind you. In his and Donald Trump's first term, the Liberal prime minister's government successfully renegotiated the North American free trade agreement that Trump was threatening to tear up. You could argue that the Mexicans did most of the heavy lifting, or that the agreement was fatally flawed by a sunset clause that meant it would have to be perpetually revisited, but a win is a win. And the government inked trade accords that Stephen Harper's Conservative government had launched with Europe and with Pacific nations.

The Liberals could also point to success in handling the COVID-19 pandemic. Massive stimulus programs preserved jobs and the economy during the critical opening months; lockdowns limited the spread of the disease; and unrelenting efforts by the federal government, accompanied by an open chequebook, secured early supplies of vaccines. Canada had one of the lowest mortality rates from the pandemic of any country in North America or Europe—an impressive accomplishment.

The Trudeau government also dedicated itself to improving the lives and sovereignty of Indigenous peoples. And it achieved the major social reform of providing a stronger safety net for delivering childcare, which improved the lives of thousands of young Canadians and significantly reduced child poverty.

The rest of Trudeau's track record, however, is so unimpressive that he is likely to be ranked one of Canada's least successful prime ministers. As evidence, let's look at those three core tasks.

✣

First: keep the economy moving. Justin Trudeau's Liberals crafted an industrial policy that identified economic sectors in need of support and created investment vehicles to provide that support. There were the Infrastructure Bank, Invest in Canada, and the Canadian Business Growth Fund. There were the Innovation Superclusters Initiative and participation in the Asian development banks. Most of these failed to live up to their much-touted potential.

Meanwhile, the government seemed hell-bent on undermining natural resource development, a critical pillar of the Canadian economy. Environmental reviews got tougher, regulations stricter. There were moratoriums on oil tanker traffic and an emissions cap on the oil and gas sector. At the same time, the government poured millions in subsidies into declining media while trying to force Facebook and Google to follow suit. Google reluctantly agreed, but Meta simply pulled news off Facebook and Instagram. The effort did more harm than good to newspapers and broadcasters. It seemed the Trudeau government was determined to subsidize troubled or undeveloped parts of the economy while punishing anything that was doing well.

Through all of this, the government ran deficits—big ones before the pandemic, massive ones during it, and big ones once again after it was over. Progressive commentators praised the government for subsidizing childcare spaces and for new dental care and pharmacare programs. But those programs were paid for with borrowed money. Meanwhile, Canada's global competitiveness steadily eroded. Trudeau's government spent lavishly but built little of enduring value, leaving the economy fragile and ill-equipped to face future challenges. The federal Liberals resembled doctors in medieval times who believed the only remedy for any ill was to bleed the patient with leeches. For the Grits, the only remedy for any ill was to increase spending.

Inflation and interest rates soared—partly due to global post-pandemic forces, partly due to federal government spending—while unemployment rose and housing became so unaffordable that it appears that many young Canadians will never enjoy what every generation since the Second World War enjoyed: a secure, well-paying job and an affordable home appreciating in value and financed by an affordable mortgage. And in 2025, Canada's productivity growth—at its most basic level, the amount produced by each worker—was the worst of any member state of the Organisation for Economic Co-operation and Development, with no prospects for improvement over the next forty years.

In short, the Trudeau years became synonymous with higher costs, diminished prospects, and a government increasingly disconnected from the realities of everyday Canadians.

Second: keep the country together. For a decade, Stephen Harper's Conservatives led a peaceful nation. After the traumas and tumult of the failed Meech Lake and Charlottetown accords, the rise of the Western protest Reform Party, the near-death experience of the 1995 referendum on Quebec sovereignty, the Supreme Court reference, and the Clarity Act, Harper decided to lower the temperature by practising a form of passive federalism. On his watch, the federal government limited itself to operating within its constitutional spheres of jurisdiction—foreign affairs, defence, justice, federal fiscal policy, transfers—and let the provinces operate unhindered within theirs: health, education, municipalities, and the like. After ten years of passive federalism, the Bloc Québécois was virtually extinct as a sovereigntist federal party, the sovereigntist Parti Québécois had been defeated provincially, Western representation and influence in Ottawa was robust, and the federation was at peace.

Justin Trudeau wanted none of that. He was a classical Canadian Liberal, believing that the federal government should use its spending power to forge programs that were in the national interest. There would be more money for health care, but only if the provinces spent the extra funds on federal priorities, such as mental health. There would be more money for childcare spaces, but only if the provinces agreed to spend most of the money on licensed, not-for-profit centres.

The provinces howled at all these intrusions. But they did more than howl. By the time Trudeau left office, the Parti Québécois was leading in the provincial polls. In the West, both the Alberta and Saskatchewan governments had passed sovereignty acts, declaring the federal power *persona non grata* in their spheres of jurisdiction. Under Trudeau, national unity was as dangerously divided as in the 1990s. Only now the West was as estranged from the Centre as Quebec had ever been.

Third: handle the Americans. In some ways, the world conspired against Justin Trudeau. His Liberals came to power at a time when economies were growing in developed nations, interest rates were low, and a friendly Democrat, Barack Obama, occupied the White House, with former secretary of state Hillary Clinton likely to succeed him. These were perfect times for national experiments in social and environmental policy, and Trudeau was eager to experiment.

Then Donald Trump shocked the world by winning the 2016 presidential election, in part by vowing to rip up the North American free trade pact with Mexico and Canada, a pact that he called "the worst trade deal ever made." It wasn't, but Trump was tapping into the zeitgeist of Middle America, which had watched once-secure manufacturing jobs disappear beyond the country's borders.

As foreign affairs minister, Chrystia Freeland played a long game, refusing to commit to meeting American demands. At one level this worked: American negotiators realized Canada wasn't going to be bullied into signing just any agreement. But ultimately, it became counterproductive; Canada watched from the sidelines while Mexican and American negotiators crafted the United States–Mexico–Canada Agreement (USMCA), which we were then obliged to sign onto while wrangling only a few minor, last-minute concessions.

Still, NAFTA was rescued, and in 2000 Joe Biden defeated Trump. But peace never fully returned. The world had become a dangerous place. China sought regional domination militarily, and global domination economically. In February 2022, Russia invaded Ukraine in an effort to expunge the country. NATO nations moved rapidly to rearm—all except Canada, which mouthed platitudes about reaching the NATO floor of 2 per cent of GDP spending on defence, but took little real action. Trump returned to the presidency in 2025 vowing to put Canada in its place, and that place might be simply as another American state. In his final weeks in office, Trudeau handled the threats coming from Washington with commendable firmness, offering to renegotiate trade agreements and tighten border security while matching American tariffs with counter tariffs and vowing there was "no way in hell" Canada would accept annexation. In some ways, nothing in his prime ministership became him like the leaving of it.

But the fact remains that in terms of the economy, national unity, and Canada–U.S. relations, the Trudeau government left everything in poorer shape than they found it. And Canada's twenty-third prime minister did worse than that.

❋

In the 1960s and '70s, confronted with the robust nationalism of quietly revolutionary Quebec, English Canada struggled to summon its own sense of national identity. This was chiefly an Ontario struggle, for Atlantic Canada had its own robust sense of self, the Prairies inherited both strongly social democratic and strongly conservative identities from Eastern European and American immigration, and British Columbia was integrated within Pacific North America, known as Cascadia. The most that Laurentian English Canada was able to come up with was "Well, at least we aren't American," whatever that meant.

But in the early years of the twenty-first century, a new definition of Canada emerged, one that recognized and reflected decades of immigration from developing countries. The Canadian identity, at least on the English side, was rooted in multiculturalism. Canada was where millions of Chinese, Indian, Filipino, Haitian, Lebanese, and Nigerian people, along with those from countless other countries, lived together and thrived in the world's most cosmopolitan cities. Younger Canadians embraced this confident new Canada, celebrating it along with the many gold medals the country—once a perpetual runner-up—won at the 2010 Winter Olympic games.

Trudeau took things much further. "There is no core identity, no mainstream in Canada," the prime minister told the *New York Times* in 2015. "There are shared values—openness, respect, compassion, willingness to work hard, to be there for each other, to search for equality and justice. Those qualities are what make us the first post-national state." This was all true, as far as it went. But how far was that? The Laurentian elite had struggled for a century and a half to build a nation based on an accommodation of identities as a means of preserving national unity, a uniquely Canadian approach to linguistic, ethnic, and regional differences within a cohesive (at least on good days) identity. Trudeau celebrated that accommodation, defining it as a utopian ideal of everyone from everywhere living happily together with no overarching identity at all.

But then Trudeau undermined that utopian ideal by substituting shame for pride in Canada's past. In truth, there were things to be ashamed of, especially the treatment of non-white and Indigenous minorities by the white majority. But at times it seemed that, for Trudeau, there was nothing *but* shame. As revelations surfaced of possible unmarked graves at former residential schools, he ordered flags on government buildings lowered to half-mast for almost six months. Six months! Not only were John A. Macdonald statues toppled by protesters who (wrongly) blamed him as the author of residential school abuses, but the Bank of Canada removed the Father of Confederation from the ten-dollar bill.

Trudeau or his ministers apologized on behalf of all Canadians: to residential school survivors, though Stephen Harper had already offered that apology in 2008; to the ghosts of the *Komagata Maru*, whose cargo of Punjabi immigrants had been turned away from Canada in May 2017; to the ghosts of the *St. Louis*, a liner filled with Jewish refugees that was turned away from Canada in 1939; to members of the LGBTQ community who had been prosecuted, persecuted, and removed from positions in the military and public service because of whom they loved; to the Inuit for their mistreatment during the tuberculosis epidemic from the 1940s to '60s; for the internment of Italian Canadians during the Second World War; for discrimination against Black soldiers during the First World War; for the killing of sled dogs in the 1950s and '60s. The Trudeau government was clear about what it disliked about Canada, but conspicuously silent about what it admired.

The country indulged in an orgy of renaming. In Ottawa, the Langevin Block, named after Macdonald's valued Quebec minister, Hector-Louis Langevin, became the generic Office of the Prime Minister and Privy Council, because Langevin had strongly supported the residential school system. The Sir John A. Macdonald Parkway became the Kichi Zībī Mīkan. In Toronto, Ryerson University became Toronto Metropolitan University—Egerton Ryerson's support for universal public education included support for residential schools—while Dundas Street almost lost its name because Henry Dundas allegedly supported slavery, even though he was in truth a fervent abolitionist. The University of Victoria converted Trutch Residence to Lansdowne Residence One because British Columbia's first lieutenant governor, Joseph Trutch, allegedly mistreated Indigenous peoples. The statue of the Earl of Cornwallis, founder of Halifax, was taken down because of his mistreatment of the Mi'kmaq. And on and on it went.

Trudeau's vision, while rhetorically progressive, failed to address a fundamental need that each of us feels for a sense of belonging, for a shared commitment that sustains a nation. Postnational idealism may have resonated in urban centres and among globalist elites, but it alienated those who saw value in Canada's distinctiveness. In their pursuit of inclusivity, the Liberals failed to grasp that unity requires more than shared values; it requires a shared sense of purpose and pride in the country's history, achievements, and potential. Without that sense of purpose, Canada risks becoming a nation in name only, fractured by competing interests and disconnected from its own story.

This is not simply a lament that things aren't what they used to be. The loss of confidence in Canada by Canadians is measurable. The Angus Reid Institute has been polling Canadians on their attitudes toward the country since the 1990s. In 1991, 65 per cent of Canadians agreed with the statement that they shared a "deep emotional attachment" to Canada. In 2015, when Justin Trudeau came to power, it was still at 62 per cent. By 2024, it had plummeted to 49 per cent. In 1995, 78 per cent of Canadians were "very proud" to be Canadian. That number had dropped to 52 per cent by 2016. In 2024, it reached a nadir of 34 per cent. "There are lots of threads pulling on the fabric of Canadian society or what we once thought defined Canada," Shachi Kurl, president of the Angus Reid Institute, told the *National Post*.[1]

This postnational ethos was also reflected in the Trudeau government's policies. Expanding immigration, implementing anti-racism initiatives, resettling refugees, and prioritizing reconciliation with Indigenous peoples were central to the Trudeau agenda, along with strong commitments to gender equity, LGBTQ rights, and climate action. While these policies resonated with urban progressives in the city centres of Central Canada and British Columbia, they clashed with cultural and economic realities. The most intense expression of that clash was the Trudeau carbon tax.

The national carbon price epitomized the Trudeau Liberals' approach to governance: it was politically calculating and deeply divisive. Although many environmentalists praised it as a vital tool in the struggle to reduce carbon emissions, other Canadians vilified the tax as a direct attack on their livelihood and cultural identity. For many in the West, the carbon tax reminded them of Pierre Trudeau's National Energy Program, enacted in 1980, an exercise in federal overreach still seared into Prairie memory for its disproportionate harm to resource-reliant provinces in favour of Central Canada. For Western Canadians, the carbon tax wasn't about climate change, it was about control. The policy symbolized the federal government's disregard for their economic backbone, the resource sector, and their cultural identity, which is so deeply tied to that industry. Prairie voters looked upon the tax as a tool of federal dominance, reigniting calls for provincial autonomy and even fuelling separatist sentiment.

(It was telling that Mark Carney's first act as prime minister was to eliminate the consumer carbon tax. That many of the beaming ministers standing behind him as he made the announcement were the same ministers who sat in the cabinet that imposed the tax in the first place was an irony that seemed lost on many voters in suburban Central Canada.)

The carbon tax underscored the essential hypocrisy of Trudeau's view of the country. He described it as a post-national mélange unified by shared commitments to values of environmental concern, cultural awareness, and inclusivity of minorities, which just happened to be his values as well. But anyone who did not share those values did not belong in his Canada. People who used guns to hunt for recreation or to protect their livestock were not part of his Canada, and his government sought to restrict those weapons' use, even though the real threat lay in handguns illegally smuggled into Canada and wielded by urban gangs.

And Canadians who protested the government's pandemic measures, especially vaccine mandates required for workplaces, transportation, and restaurants, earned his scorn. He did not recognize his opponents as loyal Canadians protesting what they saw as intrusive state interference. For him they were a "fringe minority" who held "unacceptable views."[2] He often accused the Conservatives of seeking to polarize debates with extreme rhetoric. But as often as not, he was the one doing the polarizing.

This is, we must point out, as far removed from the Conservative approach to nation-building as it is possible to get. Stephen Harper, despite his dour pragmatism, had a very romantic view of Canada, one that emphasized its past as a proud dominion within the British Empire. He reinstated the "Royal" designation in the military, restored the Queen's portrait in government buildings, and celebrated Canada's historical contributions in both world wars. This was an incomplete vision, for it was one that most Quebecers and most younger Canadians would never share. Yet if Harper's identity project lacked the cohesion needed to rally the entire nation, at least he was celebrating Canada rather than apologizing for it.

History will doubtless compare the Harper decade with the Trudeau decade. That comparison will not favour Trudeau. The Conservative prime minister, whatever his flaws, provided a stable and pragmatic model of governance. His tenure avoided the deep fractures stoked by Trudeau's postnational vision. By the end of Harper's era, Canada was a country in motion: economically confident, regionally balanced, and united under a functional federal structure. In contrast, Trudeau's legacy is one of disarray. He left the country fractured, indebted, economically adrift, and under threat from an expansionist American regime. What began as a promise of transformation ended as a cautionary tale of ambition unmoored from accountability, leaving Canada more divided and vulnerable when he left office than when he arrived.

Pierre Poilievre should have been able to ride the voter anger at the Trudeau agenda into government. But along came Donald Trump and his threatened annexation of the country. For many voters, the Conservative leader came across as Trump Lite. At the least, they doubted his ability to contain the challenges coming from Washington. They turned to a former central banker instead.

But Mark Carney assumed the leadership of a country burdened with soaring debt, the legacy of rampant inflation, a housing crisis, and deepening regional grievances. He must not only deal with the challenge of American tariffs; he must also rebuild the nation's economic foundation, restore national unity, rebalance relations with the United States, and redefine a shared identity that can hold Canadians together. The stakes are nothing less than the survival of the country.

TWO

TOO MANY PEOPLE

There are plenty of candidates for Greatest Invention of the Twentieth Century. Some would nominate penicillin, the first of the wave of antibiotics that cured once-deadly diseases. The airplane is surely a contender, evolving from the rickety biplane that managed to be airborne for twelve seconds and thirty-six metres at Kittyhawk in 1903 into the thousands of jet-powered aircraft that now cross the skies daily today. Others might name the computer, and the vast changes to information processing it brought about.

We would nominate a different candidate: the suburb.

In 1945, with the end of war, planners worried about a return of the high unemployment and economic decline that had plagued North America during the Great Depression of the 1930s. To prevent that outcome, governments in Washington

and Ottawa introduced a suite of measures aimed at easing
the return of military veterans into society. One of those measures included low-interest loans for new homes. During the
war, the Wartime Housing Ltd., a Canadian crown corporation, constructed tens of thousands of cheap, sixty-five- or
seventy-five-square-metre, two- and three-bedroom units for
workers and veterans. The Central (now Canada) Housing
and Mortgage Corporation took over operations in 1946;
it allowed rent to be used as a down payment for purchase.
The CMHC acquired tracts of land on the outskirts of cities
and built hundreds of thousands of houses that were sold
cheaply to veterans, with twenty-five-year mortgages backed
by the corporation.

War also advanced the technology of the automobile—
automatic transmission, plastics, improved methods in mass
manufacturing—making it possible for young couples to
buy on the edge of the city and for the husband (typically)
to commute by car to work. Millions left their farms or vil-
lages or urban tenements for homes with reliable heat and
central plumbing and backyards for the kids—many, many
kids, the boomer generation—to play in. The suburb was
both the incubator and the heart of the new, modern, affluent,
television-addicted middle class, an expansion of prosperity
unseen in human history. Nothing else in the twentieth century mattered for most people more than the postwar increase
in the overall standard of living exemplified by the middle-
class suburb.

The suburb continues to dominate urban life today.
According to the latest edition of the *Canadian Suburbs Atlas*,
two thirds of Canadians live in one. In the largest cities,

80 per cent of the population is suburban. For every person added to the population of a city centre, four are added to its suburbs. We are a suburban nation, becoming more suburban by the day. Progressive elites living in downtowns deride the vast swaths of mostly low-density housing that surround Canadian cities. They accuse suburban developments of taking valuable farmland out of production. They believe suburbs enslave their residents to the automobile, that they promote conformity and mediocrity of thought. For the Laurentian elite, suburbs are something they have to drive through to get to the cottage. As much as possible, they try to avoid any further contact. But at both the provincial and federal level, the suburbs elect the government. Our politicians are suburban; our governments, suburban; our outlook, suburban.

In most Canadian provinces, a conservative party of one stripe or another dominates in rural ridings while a progressive party dominates the city centres, and the two fight over the suburban voters who end up choosing the government. If times are good, suburban voters may support downtown-centred political parties that emphasize social and environmental concerns. If economic issues are top of mind, suburban voters tend to side with their conservative rural cousins. Because economic concerns are often the greatest concern, conservatives generally do somewhat better than progressives at the provincial level. Since 1960, in British Columbia, either the Social Credit Party or the Liberal Party (which contained both progressive and conservative elements) has won thirteen elections; the NDP has won five. In Manitoba, the Conservatives and the NDP have shared power about equally, but in Ontario, the Progressive Conservatives have been in government about two thirds of the time. In Quebec, parties to the right of the sovereigntist Parti Québécois have governed for forty-five of those sixty-five years.

In federal elections since 1960, though party identities have shifted and merged over the decades, Liberals have been strong in Quebec and in the city centres of Ontario and British Columbia. Various conservative parties have mostly controlled the Prairie provinces, rural Ontario, and the interior of British Columbia, while New Democrats have competed with the Liberals in the downtowns. (For the purposes of this broad comparison, we are setting aside anomalies, such as the NDP surge in Quebec in 2011, or the Liberal control of rural Ontario in the 1990s, when the Progressive Conservative and Reform parties split the right-of-centre vote.)

The real kingmaker in federal elections has been the 905—the broad band of suburban cities surrounding Toronto, named after the area code it was given in 1993. The 905 tends to vote as a bloc, and its millions of voters and two dozen seats elect both the Ontario and federal governments. In every election since Lester Pearson came to power in 1963, the suburban ridings surrounding downtown Toronto have voted more or less in sync for the party that formed government. The one exception was in 2006, when Stephen Harper's Conservatives won a weak minority government with little representation in the 905. But that representation strengthened in the election of 2008, and the Tories owned the 905 in the 2011 election that delivered them a majority.

Similarly, Justin Trudeau's Liberals took the 905 away from the Conservatives in 2015 in a majority-government victory, and held onto it in 2019 and 2021, which proved enough to secure two minority governments. Mark Carney's surge from behind that delivered victory on April 28, 2025, was powered in part by victories in Greater Toronto. The New Democrats have never been competitive in the 905. But they have won seats in suburban ridings in British Columbia's Lower Mainland. The New Democrats have traditionally been strong in B.C., although in 2025 voters largely abandoned the party, defeating NDP leader Jagmeet Singh in his seat of Burnaby South. In most other respects, the Lower Mainland politically reflects Toronto and the 905. In that sense, suburban Vancouver and the 905 generally elect the federal government together.

In the early postwar years, Canada's suburbs were as white as the country itself. In 1947, Mackenzie King repealed the Chinese Exclusion Act that his Liberal government had enacted in 1923, though King told the House of Commons: "The people of Canada do not wish, as a result of mass immigration, to make a fundamental alteration to the character of our population. Large-scale immigration from the orient would change the fundamental composition of the Canadian population."[1] But John Diefenbaker's Progressive Conservative government, through an order-in-council, banned racial discrimination in selecting immigrants. Lester Pearson's Liberals codified that measure through the creation of the points system, still in use today, which selects immigrants based on their qualifications and their ability to adapt and contribute to Canadian society. Brian Mulroney's Progressive Conservative government opened the floodgates in the early 1990s by proposing that 250,000 immigrants be admitted to Canada each year. Jean Chrétien's and Paul Martin's Liberals, and Stephen

Harper's Conservatives, held to that target. By 2010, Canada was importing the equivalent of one Toronto every ten years; one Canadian in five was not born in Canada. The vast majority of new arrivals came from China, India, and the Philippines, the top three source countries, along with other developing countries. White, Atlantic Canada was increasingly becoming brown, Pacific Canada.

In times past, many immigrants arrived impoverished, their only housing option downtown tenements. But those tenements are gone, and today's immigrants often arrive with more resources. Like the native-born, most prefer to live in suburbs. Forty-three per cent of the population of Surrey, part of Greater Vancouver, was born overseas; 33 per cent of the population of 518,000 is South Asian. In the 905, South Asians also dominate in Brampton, while just under 30 per cent of the population of Richmond Hill is of Chinese origin. Markham is Canada's most diverse city, with 82 per cent of its population a visible minority.

Conventional wisdom holds that immigrant voters support the Liberal Party because the Liberal Party supports immigrants. But immigrants from countries such as India and the Philippines are often more economically and culturally conservative overall than the native-born. They can and should be part of the Conservative governing coalition. Stephen Harper won them over, before foolishly pandering to the Tories' white, rural base during the 2015 election by criticizing women wearing the hijab and by talking about "barbaric cultural practices."

Such Tory talk, coupled with general weariness following a decade of Conservative rule, turned suburban immigrant voters back to the Liberals. For almost a decade, suburban voters in the 905 stayed there, contradicting *The Big Shift*'s assertion that they were fundamentally conservative in nature. In the election of 2021, the Liberals won just under 33 per cent of the vote, the smallest plurality for a party that won government in Canadian history. What saved them was their domination in the 905 and the suburban Lower Mainland. Not only were the suburbs not joining the Conservative coalition, they were the only thing keeping the Liberals in power. For that, the Conservatives had only themselves to blame. The Liberals successfully branded Conservative leader Andrew Scheer, in the 2019 election, as a social conservative with American citizenship who had no plan to combat global warming. His successor, Erin O'Toole, failed to support vaccine mandates at a time when the COVID-19 virus was claiming thousands of Canadian lives. Both Scheer and O'Toole lost the 905 and the Lower Mainland, even though they won the popular vote overall.

Pierre Poilievre had a much clearer grasp of suburban priorities. And he won the Conservative leadership at a time when suburban voters were turning away from the Liberals, frightened by the impact of inflation and housing costs. The Conservative coalition of the West and the suburbs was always available to any Conservative leader capable of creating it. Poilievre was that leader. Right up until the time that Justin Trudeau resigned, suburban voters were ready to vote for him. Only fear of Donald Trump drove them to support Mark Carney. Even so, Conservatives prevailed in a handful of 905 and Lower Mainland ridings, limiting Carney to a minority government.

Now Carney must try to fix an immigration system that his predecessor broke. The damage that Justin Trudeau inflicted on that system, and on public confidence in it, marks his single greatest failure as prime minister.

✿

During the 2015 election campaign, Trudeau promised to bring in twenty-five thousand refugees displaced by the civil war in Syria, and he proved better than his word: by the end of 2016, more than forty-four thousand Syrian refugees had arrived in Canada. Though most fitted in well, some brought with them the mindset that has bred so much conflict in the Middle East.

This is nothing new. For as long as Canada has been accepting immigrants, they have imported controversies from their homelands with them. Among the first settlers of what is now Ontario were Americans who had remained loyal to the Crown during the American revolution. From those loyalists evolved a strain of anti-Americanism that became a part of the national fabric. Irish immigrants in the mid-1800s, both Protestant and Catholic, carried with them the troubles of their homeland. Eastern Europeans fleeing domination by the Soviet Union after the Second World War became some of the most staunchly anti-communist hardliners in the land.

It should surprise no one, then, that recent waves of immigrants also import tensions from their homelands. Many Chinese immigrants who came to Canada from Hong Kong in the 1990s resolutely opposed the Communist regime; more recent immigrants from the mainland are generally less hostile

to Beijing. Sikhs came to Canada, in part, to escape persecution by India's Hindu majority. Many of the more recent new
arrivals from India are themselves Hindu, and many are more
supportive of the Indian government in general and Prime
Minister Narendra Modi in particular. As with earlier waves,
the children of these Indian and Chinese and Filipino and
Arab newcomers will in all likelihood show less interest in the
politics of their parents' homelands, melding into the multicultural matrix of Canadian society.

But something is going on today that never went on before.
Foreign governments are actively interfering in Canadian
politics. The Beijing government operated so-called police
stations in Toronto, Montreal, and Vancouver that gathered
intelligence on, as well as harassed and intimidated, Chinese
Canadians, especially those who are critical of the People's
Republic. Chinese interference in recent Canadian elections
was so blatant that the Trudeau government, reluctantly and
under intense pressure, ordered a public inquiry. In her final
report, released in January 2025, Commissioner Marie-Josée
Hogue concluded that foreign powers may have successfully
influenced the outcome of elections in certain ridings, although
"there is no evidence to suggest that our institutions have been
seriously affected by such interference." Nonetheless, she criticized the federal government for a lack of coordination and
communication when faced with such threats, saying it was
"insufficiently transparent when it comes to foreign interference."[2] In other words, foreign governments in general and
the Chinese in particular have failed to successfully influence
our politics, but Ottawa has done a poor job of detecting and
deterring that influence.

Indian interference in Canadian affairs has been deadly. The Canadian government expelled diplomats from India after Justin Trudeau publicly revealed that agents from that country were behind the assassination in June 2023 of Hardeep Singh Nijjar, a Canadian citizen and vocal supporter of the Khalistan movement, which advocates for an independent Sikh state.

Most worrying of all are the frightening levels of antisemitism that have appeared on Canadian streets and on the campuses of our universities. The demonstrations, protests, and encampments are ostensibly in reaction to Israel's invasion of Gaza in the wake of the horrific killings and hostage-taking of Jewish citizens by Hamas fighters on October 7, 2023. But even before the Hamas attacks, antisemitism was on the rise in Canada. According to Statistics Canada, hate crimes rose by 27 per cent between 2020 and 2021, following a 37 per cent increase the year before. Jews were by far the most common target of attack, with 145 incidents per 100,000 people. Muslims came in a very far distant second, with eight incidents per 100,000.

Three factors could be fuelling this antisemitic wave. According to Statistics Canada, the Arab population in Canada increased by 254 per cent between 2001 and 2021, the largest proportional increase for any racialized community coming into Canada. Shimon Fogel, chief executive officer of the Centre for Israel and Jewish Affairs, observes that people who are taught in Middle Eastern classrooms that Israel is the root of all evil may be receptive to antisemitic messages when they come to Canada. "I don't think it is universal, but certainly within the ideologically driven, Islamist ranks of the community, evidence of hate, from the pulpit to the grassroots level, is clearly present," he said in 2023.[3]

To repeat for the umpteenth time: It is not in any way antisemitic to criticize the Israeli government's invasion of Gaza, its assault on Hezbollah in Lebanon, its incursions in the West Bank, its efforts to eliminate Iran's nuclear weapons program. Millions of Israelis strongly oppose the policies of Likud prime minister Benjamin Netanyahu. But to deny the right of the Jews to live in their homeland is Jew hatred. To chant "From the river to the sea, Palestine shall be free," which commonly means eradicating the state of Israel, is Jew hatred. To hold the Jews of Canada accountable for the actions of the Israeli government is Jew hatred. And there is much Jew hatred in Canada.

Many of the keffiyeh-wearing protesters shouting "Free, Free Palestine!" on Canadian streets were not of Arab or Muslim background. They had not been indoctrinated with antisemitic beliefs in schools in the Middle East. They learned their antisemitism in Canadian classrooms. Anti-Zionism is now fashionably progressive within many programs at Canadian universities.

Critical race theory is based on a very sound premise. Anyone with eyes to see and ears to hear knows that racist beliefs are deeply entrenched in all societies, Canada included. People whose skin is not white have faced and still face prejudice. Canada's treatment of Indigenous people deserves the condemnation it has earned. Women have had to fight, and fight still, for something approaching equality with men. Sexual and gender minorities have been historically persecuted and face stigma and prejudice today. Racism, sexism, homophobia, and transphobia are, unhappily, very much part of Canadian society.

But for some people, including some academics, Canada is nothing *but* racism and other forms of oppression. It is an illegitimate, white, colonial, genocidal, apartheid state, committing the same atrocities on Indigenous and racialized people that they allege Israel commits on Palestinians, if not on quite the same scale. Many students, professors, and activists are not simply demonstrating solidarity with Palestinian Arabs when they take to the streets; they are also showing their opposition to, as they put it, "so-called Canada."

These new-fashioned social crusaders are joined in their protests by old-fashioned bigots who believe that Jews and Muslims and First Nations and everyone else not Christian and white are inferior. Right now, it is convenient for them to march in support of the Palestinians. But they would just as happily march against them. There are, of course, pro-Palestinian parades and demonstrations that have in their ranks those who care deeply about Palestinian suffering, especially in Gaza, and want it to end. But often, these demonstrations take on a threatening tone, especially as it concerns Jewish Canadians, fuelled by an unholy combination of those who are virulently anti-Zionist and even pro-Hamas and the terror they carry out.

Muslims also suffer from hatred in Canada. They have died at the hands of hatred in a mosque in Quebec City, on a street corner in London. Intolerance is on the rise in Canada and few escape. And the Trudeau government greatly worsened the situation.

❦

"Diversity is our strength," Trudeau loved to say. But that simply isn't true. Diversity is a challenge. When well managed, it can make us stronger. Managed poorly, which is how the Liberals managed it, diversity leaves us weaker. From the time they took office, the Liberals made increasing immigration levels a priority. The pandemic forced a temporary cutback, but by 2022 the government was roaring toward a target of five hundred thousand new permanent residents a year, twice the level accepted under previous Conservative and Liberal governments.

Long before then, things had started to go wrong. Canada had an agreement with the United States, known as the Safe Third Country Agreement, which called for each country to reject asylum claims by people entering from the other's country. But that agreement only applied to border crossings. Economic migrants fleeing hardship from countries such as Haiti and Nigeria began crossing from the United States into Canada away from border crossings and then filing asylum claims. Many of them chose an unofficial crossing at Roxham Road, about fifty kilometres south of Montreal. In 2014, the last full year of the Stephen Harper government, Immigration, Refugees and Citizenship Canada processed 7,310 asylum claims. By 2019, that figure had climbed above 64,000, a nine-fold increase. Part of the reason was a tweet.

On January 28, 2017, the day after Donald Trump signed an executive order banning refugees and travellers from several Muslim-majority countries, Trudeau tweeted: "To those fleeing persecution, terror & war, Canadians will welcome you, regardless of your faith. Diversity is our strength #WelcomeToCanada." Before that tweet, border officials stopped about 315 people per month from crossing illegally; after the tweet, about 18,000 people crossed irregularly in 2017 and claimed asylum.

The Canadian and American governments eventually agreed to apply the Safe Third Country Agreement across the entire border. But claimants kept coming, quadrupling the backlog of pending cases. Asylum claimants were forced to wait four years for their case to be heard. But maybe "forced" is the wrong word. While they waited, claimants received publicly funded health care and work permits. For anyone fleeing poverty or violence in a developing country, the prospect of four years in Canada could be enormously attractive, especially when that period could be extended through appeals. If all else failed, the claimant might simply disappear from government view.

But the asylum claims mess wasn't the worst of it—not by a long shot. In the wake of the pandemic, employers warned of looming labour shortages. To meet those shortages, the federal government allowed employers to bring in as many temporary foreign workers (TFWs) as they needed. The country was flooded with workers taking jobs that native-born Canadians didn't want or wouldn't accept at the pay being offered. This has always been the case in some sectors, such as agriculture, but now TFWs were working at Amazon, Tim Hortons, and other big chains.

The government wasn't done yet. For decades, Canada has welcomed international students, whose high tuition fees help buttress the bottom lines of cash-strapped universities and colleges. Domestic undergraduate students pay, on average, around $7,000 a year for tuition; international students

pay on average $38,000. These students also have a preferred
path to permanent resident status, as they should—after all,
they're well educated and proficient in an official language,
and they're young, which means they'll pay taxes for decades
before collecting pensions or accessing health care and other
government services used by older folk. To help pay for tuition and living costs, students were permitted to work twenty
hours a week. In 2022, the Liberals decided to eliminate most
work restrictions. Immediately, things spiralled out of control.

International students became part of the stream of temporary foreign workers. Although the universities for the
most part behaved, some colleges became incredibly aggressive in recruiting students. Conestoga College in Kitchener,
Ontario, doubled its student population to forty-five thousand, with international students far outnumbering domestic
students. Bogus private colleges popped up, offering bogus
diplomas—Immigration Minister Marc Miller called them
"puppy mills"—while shady immigration consultants, particularly in India, lured students with promises of jobs and
citizenship in Canada.

By the beginning of 2023, there were 2.5 million international students and temporary foreign workers in Canada,
accounting for 6.5 per cent of Canada's population. The
Statistics Canada report announcing those numbers appeared
to surprise the federal government as much as the rest of the
population. There were an estimated five hundred thousand
illegal immigrants ("undocumented" is the preferred term in
polite society, but the fact is, they are in the country without
a permit, and that's illegal), a combination of asylum seekers whose claims had been refused and temporary workers

and international students who didn't leave after their permits expired. The newcomers contributed to skyrocketing rent increases and housing shortages. They contributed to unemployment, which has been trending up since the pandemic, reaching 6.9 per cent in April 2025, the highest level since 2017. They contributed as well to lagging productivity, since employers preferred hiring cheap foreign workers to investing in automation. None of this, it must be stressed, is the fault of the students and workers; it is the fault of poorly thought-out federal policies.

In a panic, the Liberals backtracked in 2024, announcing reductions in the number of international students allowed into the country and in the hours they could work. The government also capped and reduced temporary foreign worker permits and the targets for permanent residents. Justin Trudeau even put out a video. It was a vintage performance. Perched on the edge of a comfortable chair, sleeves rolled up, he offered a friendly but also condescending explanation of his government's latest policy failure. Although he admitted "we made some mistakes," he blamed the out-of-control increases on "bad actors, like fake colleges and big-chain corporations."[4] This was an astonishing, if unsurprising, admission of how little Trudeau understands or cares about the private sector. "Big-chain corporations," like all businesses, seek capable workers at the lowest possible wage. If the federal government offers them qualified foreigners willing to work for a lower wage than many native-born will accept, they will take advantage of the program. They are not the bad actors; the government that made the workers available to them was the one acting badly.

❧

Since 1976, the Environics Institute has been polling Canadians on their attitude toward immigration. The results in 2024 were grim. "For the first time in a quarter century, a clear majority of Canadians say there is too much immigration," the report concluded, "with this view strengthening considerably for the second consecutive year."[5]

Before we explore why attitudes toward immigration have changed, let's look briefly at how they changed in the past. In 1976, when Environics first began its survey, 61 per cent of Canadians felt that there was too much immigration in Canada, while 35 per cent disagreed. Those numbers stayed more or less constant through the 1980s. Some Canadians worried that the country's British and French cultural bases were being undermined, that the newcomers would not assimilate. This has always been the attitude of some native-born toward new arrivals, from Irish Catholics to Eastern Europeans to Chinese and Indians and Filipinos. Each new wave of immigrants has proved the skeptics wrong. Another factor was also at work. Canada's economy struggled in the 1970s to overcome the global impacts of stagflation: high inflation and stagnant growth, brought on in part by rising oil prices and monetary policies that accepted inflation in order to combat unemployment, worsening both. The 1980s began with a crippling recession, followed by the beginnings of a sustained economic recovery.

In the 1990s, as central banks finally brought inflation under control, as governments wrested their deficits into balance, and as benefits of the 1988 free trade agreement with the

United States began working their way through the economy, growth took off. By now, as well, it was clear the immigrants from the developing world were integrating into, and contributing to, Canadian society. Opposition to immigration steadily decreased. As the millennium turned, more Canadians supported immigration than opposed it, even though Canada was bringing in 250,000 people a year—far more, per capita, than the United States or the members of the European Union. In 2021, 69 per cent of Canadians supported the federal government's generous immigration policies, while only 27 per cent opposed it, a complete reversal from the 1970s and '80s.

For three decades now, immigration has been Canada's secret weapon. Fertility rates are falling around the world. Many developed and some developing countries are in population decline. But Canada has been able to sustain its population, and slow population aging, by bringing in hundreds of thousands of newcomers every year who generate growth and prosperity, with little of the social friction that other countries have faced. We have been the very best at inducing the very best to come to our shores. And the vast, peaceful polyglot suburbs where most of us live became their home. When diversity is the result of policies handled thoughtfully and well, it truly is our strength.

And then the pandemic struck, even as the Trudeau government allowed unprecedented numbers of permanent residents, temporary workers, international students, and asylum seekers to enter Canada. Suddenly, it was 1976 all over again. The 2024 Environics study showed no evidence of Canadians suddenly becoming racist or intolerant. Instead, people worried about the strain that too many newcomers were putting

on the housing and rental market, and on health care and other
social services. They worried that low-wage foreign workers
were undercutting native-born workers in the job market.
They worried that the government was doing a poor job of
screening newcomers, some of whom might embrace extremist ideologies. They believed that many asylum claimants were
not real refugees, fleeing violence and persecution, but simply
economic migrants abusing the system.

It is true that the Environics survey noted a sharp uptick
in those who believed that "too many immigrants do not
adopt Canadian values." But the main reason so many Canadians now believe there are too many immigrants coming
into the country is that *there are too many immigrants coming into the country.* This is not an anti-immigrant sentiment.
It's a predictable reaction to the botched immigration policies
of the Trudeau government. This is when diversity becomes
our weakness.

We have another good yardstick by which to judge whether
intolerance is on the rise in Canada. The closest thing this
country has to the anti-immigrant, far-right policies you see
in the American MAGA movement that helped bring Donald
Trump back as president, or that are on the rise across Europe,
is the People's Party of Canada, led by former Conservative cabinet minister Maxime Bernier. This fringe party was
unpopular from the get-go. In the 2019 federal election, it
scored 1.6 per cent of the popular vote. But when the pandemic struck, Bernier appeared to be riding a bit of a ripple.
He opposed lockdowns, vaccine mandates, and masks while
calling for cuts to immigration and, for good measure, limits
to transgender rights. In the 2021 federal election, he more

than doubled his share of the popular vote, to 4.6 per cent. But then Pierre Poilievre became Conservative leader and managed to draw much of Bernier's support back into the Conservative tent. In the 2025 election, the PPC was down to 0.7 per cent of the vote, an extinction event.

Pierre Poilievre has been vague about immigration policy, saying that it should be brought down to a sustainable level. "We have to slow down the numbers," he told Jordan Peterson, the controversial psychology professor and conservative commentator, in December 2024. He claimed he would end the abuse of the international student and temporary worker programs while also putting an end to demonstrations and clashes on Canadian streets based on home-country grievances. "Bring your traditions and your culture and your stories," he said, "but leave the problems at the door."[6] For his part, Mark Carney promised during the election campaign to maintain the lower levels belatedly established by the Trudeau government.

Restoring public confidence in the value and importance of immigration—especially the confidence of voters in the suburbs, many of whom are immigrants—will be one of Carney's greatest challenges. Justin Trudeau's overenthusiasm for immigration, multiculturalism, and diversity has brought the immigration system to the breaking point. It's up to the Liberals now to fix what they broke.

THREE

DUELLING ALIENATIONS

In January 2025, Justin Trudeau and Canada's premiers met to discuss how to respond to president-elect Donald Trump's threats of tariffs on Canadian exports. They agreed that Canada would respond forcefully, employing "a full range of measures to ensure a robust response to possible U.S. tariffs."[1] Danielle Smith was having none of it. "Alberta will simply not agree to export tariffs on our energy or other products, nor do we support a ban on exports of those same products," the premier declared on X, the former Twitter. "We will take whatever actions are needed to protect the livelihoods of Albertans from such destructive federal policies."[2]

Smith feared that in any trade war between Canada and the United States, a Liberal government would be prepared to sacrifice the Alberta economy by taxing or restricting oil

and gas exports. Although during the federal election Mark
Carney promised that no region will be expected to bear
more than its fair share of the pain of counter tariffs, Smith
remained unconvinced. She issued nine demands to which any
federal government must commit to satisfy Alberta's concerns.
The most important condition was the first: "Guaranteeing
Alberta full access to unfettered oil and gas corridors to the
north, east, and west."[3]

If Canada is at a breaking point, some of the fissures are
as old as Confederation. When the newly created Canadian
federal government convinced the Hudson's Bay Company to
sell its lands to the Dominion in 1870, business interests in
Ontario and Quebec assumed the vast new territory would
serve as a de facto colony of Central Canada. Unlike the
founding provinces, the three Prairie provinces had no control
over their natural resources, which the people of those provinces bitterly resented. Even when they won that control in
1930, Prairie residents continued to harbour suspicions that
the East intended to keep some measure of control over the
West. Those fears were amply justified when Pierre Trudeau's
Liberals effectively suppressed Prairie oil prices in the early
1980s in an effort to subsidize Ontario and Quebec industries through the National Energy Program. And the despised
NEP included an export charge on oil and natural gas sold
into the United States. Prairie voters have every reason to
fear that a Liberal federal government would find some way
to restrict oil and gas exports into the United States in retali-
ation for tariffs.

Smith conducted her own diplomacy on behalf of her
province's interests, lobbying officials in Washington at

Trump's Mar-a-Lago estate and attending a Republican fundraiser during the Canadian election campaign. In one infamous photo, she posed with Trump and businessman/ television personality Kevin O'Leary, smiling in the Florida sun, sending an unmistakable signal that she was not about to play by Ottawa's rules. Her campaign may have had an effect: when Trump imposed the 25 per cent tariff, the energy-export tariff was an exception, set at 10 per cent. Further backtracking by the Trump administration offered exemptions for Canadian exports that complied with the United States–Mexico–Canada Agreement.

Canada is not a love story. It is a marriage of convenience, a survival strategy conceived a century and a half ago for a collection of colonies that were determined to protect their autonomy from America's Manifest Destiny. Since the first grand bargain of Confederation, Ottawa and the provinces have lurched about like awkward dance partners, stumbling over obstacles and arguing endlessly over who should take the lead. The result is a nation held together not by a shared vision but by barely managed tensions.

Traditionally, the greatest threat to unity has been the nationalist movement in Quebec. But as the Western provinces have grown in power and influence, and as the Laurentian elites in Central Canada have ignored or tried to control that growth, Western alienation from the Centre has deepened. The tariff threat was the latest manifestation of those divisions. If Ottawa imposed energy tariffs or restrictions, the impact on Alberta would be devastating. In 2024, Canada's oil and gas exports to the U.S. topped $150 billion, dwarfing any other sector. So Smith drew a line in the sand. Alberta would not support Ottawa's plan. The much-touted Team Canada approach was publicly and undeniably fractured.

The Laurentian Consensus is not up to the challenge of the rising West. Dealing with Quebec nationalism has long been its focus, with Western protests treated as whining complaints by regional malcontents. Central Canadians were shocked in 1993 when Preston Manning's Reform Party, a movement of Western protest, arrived in Ottawa. But when Reform merged with the Progressive Conservatives to create the new Conservative Party of Canada, Western power and influence became entrenched in the federal political scene. The Conservatives were no longer the party of Bay Street or Red Tory *noblesse oblige.* The new party was Western-based, populist, and permanent. The political centre of gravity had shifted.

Justin Trudeau's Liberal victory in 2015, after a decade of Conservative rule, helped convince the Laurentianists living in their downtown Central Canadian strongholds that they were still at the centre of political power. They turned their faces away from the West every bit as much as they turned them away from the rising power of the suburbs in their own communities. They ignored new immigration patterns that had turned Vancouver, Calgary, and Edmonton into some of the fastest-growing cities in North America. Newcomers were settling not just in the car-commuting suburbs of Toronto but also in the booming suburbs of Surrey, Airdrie, and Langley, where they built their lives around small businesses, homeownership, and family values that aligned more with the new Conservative coalition than with the progressive politics of downtown elites. This was not a temporary shift. The old Canada, where elections were won and lost in

Ontario and Quebec while the West watched from the sidelines, was fading. In its place, a new Canada was emerging, one where Western voices could no longer be dismissed as fleeting temper tantrums. They were now at the centre of the national conversation.

Then came the greatest shock of all: the transformation of the United States from protector and customer to potential adversary and competitor. In the 2025 federal election, fewer than five hundred thousand more people voted for the safety of Mark Carney than committed to Pierre Poilievre: 43.7 per cent of the popular vote, compared to 41.3 per cent. But that only left Western voters feeling even more estranged. Days later, on May 3, hundreds of Alberta separatist supporters rallied at the Edmonton legislature, even as Smith greatly lowered the threshold for citizen-initiated referendums, which could include a referendum on separation.

A nation's strength depends on the shared bonds among its people: some combination of a common language, faith, culture, and economic interests. This is why diversity can challenge Canada as well as strengthen it. The fewer things a nation's citizens have in common, the more difficult the job becomes of uniting them. And when internal cleavages align with deep geographic and jurisdictional divides, those divisions can become fault lines. Governing a nation of vast distances and differing cultural landscapes demands a clear-eyed understanding of the centrifugal forces that risk pulling the country apart. Canada's founders knew their national project was fragile. In response, they built a system designed to accommodate regional interests, recognizing that maintaining some semblance of unity would require constant effort and compromise. In contrast, today's leaders too often neglect these accommodations, substituting their own values while dismissing the concerns of others, at a perilous cost to national cohesion.

With each passing day, Canada's provinces and territories are becoming less alike. Ontario and Quebec are drifting in different directions. Atlantic Canada and Western Canada are not just on different oceans; they increasingly inhabit different realities. The energy-driven growth of Alberta and Saskatchewan, the Pacific integration of British Columbia, the aging populations of the Maritimes, and the manufacturing and service-oriented economies of Ontario and Quebec are becoming difficult to reconcile. Yet reconcile them we must, if the Canadian experiment is to endure. To get to where you want to go, you must first know where you are. For Canada, that means understanding the true nature of regional evolutions that challenge national cohesion.

ATLANTIC CANADA

First, the good news. Atlantic Canada is finally attracting its proper share of immigrants. Back in 2013, only 5,800 new permanent residents settled in Newfoundland and Labrador, Nova Scotia, New Brunswick, and Prince Edward Island. In 2023, a record 32,000 moved into the region. If that rate holds, it would mean the equivalent of delivering a new Charlottetown each year. Immigrants bring energy to the community and to the economy, and they lessen the problems of societal aging, which is particularly severe in Atlantic Canada. It isn't too much to say that immigration levels are the backbone of Atlantic Canada's future, if it has one.

Now, the mixed news. Immigration retention rates aren't what they should be. About six in ten immigrant arrivals in Nova Scotia are still there five years later. The number is about five in ten for New Brunswick. It's a bit lower than that for Newfoundland and Labrador, while only one in four stay in Prince Edward Island.

Finally, the bad news: Atlantic Canada is still not a welcoming-enough place for newcomers. There aren't enough jobs for them. There aren't the kind of family or cultural ties that they might find in Toronto or Vancouver. And, as Tony Fang, an economics professor at Memorial University, told the Canadian Press in 2024, another reason is "lack of community support."[4] The curse of being "from away" remains potent in Atlantic Canada.

Atlantic Canada also remains heavily dependent on federal transfers, with the highest level, per capita, in the country. The working-age population is shrinking, while the demand for health care is skyrocketing as retirees from other parts of the country move to the region, attracted by its beauty and comparatively low housing costs. Provincial budgets confront a relentless cycle of rising costs and diminishing revenues.

Lower levels of immigrant retention and a lack of economic opportunity that sends people down the road contribute to the region's steadily diminishing relevance. In 1960, Atlantic Canada represented 10.4 per cent of the national population. Today, that number has fallen to just 6.4 per cent, and every year it drops a little more. The region's political influence is also fading. The Atlantic provinces hold relatively few seats in the House of Commons—they would hold even fewer were it not for protections that prevent them from having seats taken away during seat redistributions following each census—and as Canada's population growth continues shifting westward, their voice in federal decision making weakens further. Ontario, Alberta, and British Columbia are gaining power while the Maritimes shrink into political irrelevance. This shift could have major consequences for the region's ability to secure the federal funding on which it has long relied.

The cycle is truly pernicious: A diminishing workforce slows economic growth, making it even harder to attract and retain new residents. As young workers leave, businesses struggle to find talent, tax revenues decline, and the region becomes even more dependent on federal transfers.

In 2024, more than $12 billion in equalization payments flowed into the region, covering a massive share of the provincial budgets: one third of the Nova Scotia budget consists of federal transfers; the figure for Prince Edward Island is almost 40 per cent. Without these transfers, provincial governments would be forced into severe austerity, cutting deeply into health care, education, and infrastructure. Despite efforts to modernize, Atlantic Canada remains tied to traditional industries that are increasingly out of step with the demands of a modern economy. Fishing, forestry, and resource extraction still dominate, but these sectors cannot deliver the sustained year-round growth needed to support a competitive workforce. Information technology and renewable energy show promise, but they lack the scale to transform the region's economic fortunes. If Atlantic Canada wants to secure its future, it must find ways to leverage its strategic location, natural resources, and well-educated workforce to build globally competitive businesses.

For years, Atlantic Canada has been a haven of affordable real estate, drawing in retirees and remote workers from other parts of Canada looking for a lower cost of living. But prices are rising fast. The average cost of a home in Halifax is half that of a home in Toronto, but prices in the city have doubled over the past decade. Local wages have not kept pace, creating affordability challenges for younger residents already burdened by student debt and limited job opportunities.

Yet for all its challenges, Atlantic Canada remains a place of resilience, community, and deep cultural identity. The region's strong sense of belonging has sustained it through economic hardship before, and its heritage continues to attract tourism and to support vibrant local industries in music, arts, and crafts. Its natural beauty and quality of life make it an appealing destination for those seeking a slower pace. These strengths, if properly harnessed, could form the foundation of a more sustainable economy and society.

One famous story points to that potential. The Hadhad family had been making chocolate in Damascus since the 1980s. The firm employed hundreds and shipped their delicious product throughout the Middle East. Then came the civil war. Members of the family were tortured and executed. The factory was bombed. The Hadhads fled to Lebanon as refugees. In 2015, they were among the tens of thousands of Syrian refugees welcomed to Canada. Community members in Antigonish raised funds to sponsor the family. The next year, the Hadhads started a new business, Peace By Chocolate. Today, it is the third largest employer in Antigonish, and its website is the largest e-commerce platform in the region.

There could be more people like the Hadhads powering the Maritimes' future. Moncton is one of the fastest-growing cities in Canada, driven largely by immigrants and people from other provinces who empower the regional economy. Safe, bilingual, and with comparatively reasonable housing costs, southeastern New Brunswick is attracting everyone from students to new permanent residents to remote workers from Central Canada.

Atlantic Canada's future depends on its ability to adapt. Attracting and retaining immigrants, fostering economic diversification, and addressing the needs of an aging population will ensure long-term prosperity. The region is at a crossroads. It can continue to rely on Ottawa's support, watching its influence wane and its communities weaken, or it can take control of its future. The latter course would be wiser. For who knows what Canada's economy will look like in the years ahead, and how much it will be able to spare for a region that appears chronically unable or unwilling to help itself?

QUEBEC

The noise was astonishing. As Team Canada prepared to face off against Team USA during the NHL's 4 Nations Face-Off at Montreal's Bell Centre on February 15, 2025, fans lustily booed "The Star-Spangled Banner." Trump's tariff threats and annexationist jibes went down in Montreal as badly as in the rest of Canada. But even more remarkable was what happened next. When it came time for "O Canada," the crowd took over the job of singing it, delivering the most passionate rendition many observers had ever heard.

Je me souviens. "I remember." Quebec's motto is more than a sticker on a licence plate. It is a pledge to safeguard the province's language, culture, and autonomy. For generations, Quebecers have fought to preserve their identity in an overwhelmingly English-speaking continent. But as Quebec moves deeper into the twenty-first century, its distinctiveness faces unprecedented challenges. Once the defining issue of Quebec politics, the sovereignty movement is in freefall. The 1995 referendum came within a whisker of success, with 49.42 per cent of Quebecers voting to break away from Canada. But a January 2025 Léger poll found that support for sovereignty had dropped to just 31 per cent. The shift is not temporary. It is generational, economic, and demographic.

At its height, sovereignty was a project of Quebec's baby boomers, fuelled by the Quiet Revolution's push for secularism, modernization, and cultural renewal. The movement sought to carve out a distinct, self-sufficient Quebec in the face of Anglo dominance. But younger Quebecers, shaped by globalization, digital interconnectedness, and economic pragmatism, do not share the same perspective. For them, independence feels outdated and unnecessary, a solution to a problem that no longer exists. Where previous generations saw sovereignty as a path to renewal, today's youth see in it only isolation. They have grown up in a Quebec deeply integrated into Canada's economy, where bilingualism is an asset, not a battleground. They are not fighting to break free, because they never felt trapped.

Could that change? We may be about to find out. The Parti Québécois has been leading other parties in the polls, and leader Paul St-Pierre Plamondon has vowed to hold a third referendum if his party wins the 2026 provincial election.

Could the prospect of that referendum galvanize younger voters, especially when confronted with the danger of an annexationist United States? Or is Quebec's cultural and linguistic security better protected within Confederation?

Old arguments for sovereignty insist on the need for Quebec's exclusive control over its hydroelectric wealth and natural resources. But today's knowledge-driven economy is more globally integrated. Would Quebecers be willing to risk jobs, investment, and economic stability for a political project that offers no clear financial upside? Quebec is already enmeshed in Canada's financial, regulatory, and trade networks. Sovereignty would mean renegotiating trade agreements, losing federal transfer payments, and destabilizing industries that rely on cross-border commerce. Quebec receives more than $13 billion annually in equalization payments from Ottawa, nearly 60 per cent of all equalization funds sent out by the federal government. A break from Canada would place those funds in jeopardy, forcing difficult fiscal choices that most Quebecers are unwilling to entertain.

Former PQ premier Lucien Bouchard famously said that sovereignty required winning conditions: an alignment of political enthusiasm, economic confidence, and public will. Today, those conditions have never been further out of reach. Quebec's share of Canada's total population has shrunk from 29 per cent in 1960 to just 22 per cent today. Meanwhile, Ontario's has grown from 34 per cent to 39 per cent, reflecting the size of its economy and its ability to attract immigrants.

Quebec is not only falling behind its Central Canadian partner; it's also aging rapidly, along with the rest of the country. The province's fertility rate of 1.38, while higher than

Ontario's 1.22, remains well below the replacement level of 2.1 births per woman, which maintains a stable population. The result is an increasing strain on health care, social services, and labour markets, with fewer young workers entering the economy to sustain growth.

Today's Quebec nationalism does not just alienate youth. It struggles to resonate with Quebec's growing immigrant population, many of whom see themselves as part of a multicultural Canada rather than as a separate Quebec nation. More than fifty thousand permanent residents come to the province each year. Although this is far lower, as a percentage, than in the fast-growing parts of Canada such as southern Ontario, urban Alberta, and B.C.'s Lower Mainland, it nonetheless accounts for virtually all population growth in the province. As immigrants alter the demographic mix, the notion of separatism further recedes.

That said, Quebec should be taking in far more immigrants than it currently accepts. The province's foreign-born population is just 15 per cent, according to the 2021 census, compared to almost 30 per cent in Ontario and British Columbia and 23 per cent in Alberta. Montreal's immigrant population stands at 24 per cent, far behind Toronto at 47 per cent, Vancouver at 42 per cent, and Calgary at 33 per cent. This puts Quebec at a major disadvantage in the race for talent, investment, and economic renewal. While other provinces aggressively compete for global talent, Quebec's immigration policies have remained defensive, prioritizing cultural protection over economic growth.

Rather than embracing immigration to offset demographic decline, Quebec has moved in the opposite direction.

Successive governments have tightened language laws, cultural restrictions, and secularism policies, making integration more difficult for newcomers. For the past two decades, Quebec has doubled down on protecting its identity. The province has also prioritized French-speaking immigrants, particularly from North Africa, to maintain its linguistic majority. The 2021 census shows that Arabs now make up 3.4 per cent of Quebec's population and Muslims account for 8.7 per cent of Greater Montreal. This shift has fuelled divisive debates over secularism and integration. The Coalition Avenir Québec government defended Bill 21, which bans public servants from wearing religious symbols such as hijabs, kippahs, and turbans, as a defence of the province's secular values. But the law disproportionately targets religious minorities. While Ontario, British Columbia, and Alberta embrace multiculturalism, Quebec has sought to control immigration to protect its cultural identity. When announcing a new bill in 2025 to promote Quebec's common culture, Immigration Minister Jean-François Roberge made it clear that because multiculturalism "doesn't define a common culture," it doesn't work for his province. "Quebec is a nation in its own right with a strong culture," he explained.[5]

The costs of this isolation from the broader Canadian society are mounting. Quebec's aging population and reliance on immigration for labour force growth make its resistance to diversity economically risky. The province's insularity threatens to alienate newcomers, discourage investment, and accelerate demographic decline. The question is no longer just whether Quebec can preserve its distinct identity, but whether its refusal to adapt will leave it economically and socially marginalized.

And now Donald Trump wants Quebec to become merely part of a fifty-first American state. The notion is ludicrous, of course, but what was true in 1864, when Quebec agreed to enter Confederation with Ontario, Nova Scotia, and New Brunswick, remains true today. Quebec can better preserve its language, culture, and autonomy within the Canadian federation than on its own in a North American English-speaking sea. That, at least, is what people in the rest of Canada tell people in Quebec. Many older Quebecers would be willing to take the risk; younger people, not so much.

But however the next referendum on sovereignty plays out—if, that is, the PQ wins power and proceeds with that referendum—the truth remains that insularity is a recipe for decline. To embrace its future, rather than cling to its past, Quebec must both protect its identity and accept the realities of a changing world.

ONTARIO

According to the Laurentian myth, Ontario is the heartland, the only province without a regional identity, the province most willing to sacrifice for the national interest, the Captain Canada province. In reality, Ontario is a region like any other, with its own grievances and challenges. And because both Liberal and Conservative governments have neglected its interests, the heartland is at risk.

The province has lost more than two hundred thousand manufacturing jobs since the beginning of the century, the work offshored to lower-wage jurisdictions. Wages have fallen below the national average. Manufacturing has fallen from 15 per cent of the Ontario economy to 9 per cent. A province that once enjoyed unemployment below the national average now has above-average unemployment. A province whose citizens once sent money to other, less fortunate, provinces through equalization first qualified for equalization payments in 2010. In 2024, it received $576 million—a paltry sum compared to Quebec's $13.53 billion, but still. . . .

A province whose robust natural resources once underpinned the rest of the economy is finding it nearly impossible to further develop those resources. The Ring of Fire, a mineral-rich region about five hundred kilometres northeast of Thunder Bay, remains undeveloped, thanks in part to the inability of the government to reach agreement with First Nations. A province that was once a matrix of communities, from small towns to medium-sized cities, with Toronto at the centre, is starting to resemble a city state: Greater Toronto and Hamilton contain more than seven million people. Conversely, communities from Chatham in the southwest to Pembroke on the Ottawa River have lost population (though both are experiencing a bit of a rebound) as branch plants have closed and people have gone in search of jobs in larger centres. Dilapidated main streets feature empty storefronts and sidewalks.

The province's population grew from eleven million at the turn of the century to sixteen million today, with most of that growth jammed into the Golden Horseshoe, along with Ottawa. All those extra people pushed up the cost of housing. In 2001, the average cost of a house in Vancouver was just under $300,000, compared to $250,000 for Toronto. In 2025, it was $1.2 million in both cities.

The suburbs grow at the expense of the downtowns. Following the 2021 census, the House of Commons increased in size from 338 seats to 343. The electoral commission that

drew up the new riding boundaries for Ontario took one seat
away from Northern Ontario and another from Toronto, while
increasing the number of seats in and around the 905. Toronto
politicians howled at the loss of representation for the city.
"As the fastest growing city and economic engine of Canada,
Toronto should have more representation, not less," protested Councillor Lily Cheng,[6] one of two dozen councillors
who signed a petition asking the boundaries commission to
restore the seat. But the commission was unmoved. Although
Toronto's population did grow between 2011 and 2021, the
population of the suburban cities grew much faster. To keep
riding populations more or less equal, the 905 needed to gain
seats. Toronto suffered the consequences.

Economically, Ontario is part of the Great Lakes region
that includes Michigan, Illinois, and New York. The heart
of that economy is the automotive and auto-parts industry.
But in the early 2000s, a commodity boom pushed up the
Canadian dollar, making exports less competitive. Improved
technologies led manufacturers to employ fewer workers. Provincial and federal governments seemed at a loss as to how to
preserve or replace manufacturing jobs. In later years, Justin
Trudeau's Liberals in Ottawa and Doug Ford's Progressive
Conservatives at Queen's Park offered $57 billion in com-
bined subsidies for new electric vehicle battery factories. And
all of that came before Donald Trump's decision to impose
tariffs on automobiles exported into the United States.

In any case, the better approach to improving productivity
and fostering economic growth is not to subsidize industries
but to invest more in the fundamentals: ensuring that Ontario
schools, colleges, and universities produce a well-educated

and adaptable workforce; financing nuclear and other green energy sources to make sure industries have plenty of clean, cheap electricity; improving roads, railroads, and public transit to move goods and people around swiftly. The greatest challenge to Ontario's economy isn't the lack of capital for automotive plants, it's the fact that the GTA has one of the worst commuting times in North America.

Ontario's future in automotive manufacturing, in advanced manufacturing, in financial and other services, and in cultural industries, lies in improving infrastructure, in giving kids a good education, and, most important, in paying its full share of the cost of properly defending Canada. The alternative is a border that gets steadily thicker, and an Ontario that grows steadily weaker.

THE WESTS

Alberta, British Columbia, Saskatchewan, and Manitoba are shaped by distinct histories, economies, and political cultures. The idea of a unified Western Canada is a convenient political construct, but the provinces often have competing interests and diverging trajectories. Alberta stands apart as the most vocal and politically assertive province in the region, fuelled by a deep belief in economic self-sufficiency and an enduring sense of grievance. Saskatchewan, with its own history of federal battles, is not far behind. British Columbia looks increasingly toward the Pacific, forging economic and cultural ties with Cascadia and with Asia. Manitoba remains politically centrist and economically diversified, balancing strong agricultural and manufacturing sectors. As we noted in *The Big Shift*, the West is really the Wests.

While the Laurentian elite obsesses over Quebec's place in Confederation, the battle for Canada's future will be fought in the Wests. No provinces embody this fight more than Alberta and Saskatchewan. Once seen as the quiet, dependable breadbasket of the country, they have become political powerhouses in their own right, demanding recognition and respect. Federal climate policies, pipeline blockages, and a taxation system that bleeds them dry have turned their anger into action. The sense of alienation only deepened under Prime Minister Justin Trudeau, whose government went out of its way—or so it seemed—to antagonize the very provinces that keep Canada's economy afloat.

Alberta has long seen itself as the economic engine of the West, powered by its vast oil and gas reserves. Energy exports have fuelled rapid growth and drawn waves of migrants from other provinces and beyond. Between 2016 and 2021, Alberta gained more interprovincial migrants than any other province except British Columbia. The province's economy is still deeply tied to oil and gas, with energy accounting for more than 25 per cent of its GDP and more than 80 per cent of its exports. But Alberta is tired of seeing its wealth siphoned off to Ottawa while being vilified for producing the very resource that keeps the country's lights on.

The carbon tax, first imposed by Trudeau's government in 2019 and increased repeatedly until finally reversed by Mark Carney, became a rallying cry for Alberta's frustration. But the province's estrangement is based not on one piece of legislation but on decades of federal intrusion into its affairs. In 2023, Premier Danielle Smith introduced the Alberta Sovereignty within a United Canada Act, a landmark piece of legislation designed to push back against federal overreach. The act was met with either anger or smug condescension by political elites in Central Canada, but it enjoyed strong support in Alberta. In the wake of the 2025 election result, Smith revised the terms for a citizen-initiated referendum that would make it easier for a grassroots movement to generate a vote on sovereignty. Let the word go out, from Bonavista to Vancouver Island: Alberta is nobody's doormat.

Pipeline blockages have been another flashpoint. The federal government's botched handling of the Trans Mountain Pipeline expansion is a case study in how not to manage national energy policy. Delays, regulatory hurdles, and political interference turned a crucial infrastructure project into a multi-billion-dollar boondoggle. Meanwhile, British Columbia's government actively opposed the project, further straining Western unity, and First Nations communities found themselves divided in support or opposition. For Alberta, and increasingly for Canada, pipelines are not just infrastructure, they are economic lifelines. That the federal government refuses to push through additional pipeline projects, while simultaneously importing oil from foreign nations with abysmal environmental records, is taken as a slap in the face by Canada's domestic oil and gas industry.

To add outrage to insult, once Donald Trump threatened to slap tariffs on oil and gas imports from Canada, albeit at a lower rate than other goods, Liberal politicians in Ottawa and even Quebec premier Philippe Couillard began musing that an all-Canadian pipeline from Alberta to New Brunswick might not be such a bad idea after all, even though years before they had effectively scuttled the Energy East proposal, which would have done exactly that.

Saskatchewan, which in the past has often been over-shadowed by Alberta's more overt resistance, has today been no less aggressive in pushing back against Ottawa. Premier Scott Moe took a hard stance against the carbon tax, refusing to collect it on home heating oil in an open act of defiance. Saskatchewan is rich in oil, gas, and potash, yet it remains shackled by federal policies designed for urban voters in Toronto and Montreal. The province is one of Canada's largest food exporters, yet it faces constant regulatory interference from Ottawa bureaucrats who have probably never set foot on a Saskatchewan farm. Saskatchewan under Moe passed a sovereignty act of its own.

Both Alberta and Saskatchewan contribute billions more to the federal government than they receive in return. In 2024, Alberta's net contribution to federal revenues was estimated at $20 billion, while Quebec remained the largest recipient of equalization payments, receiving $13.5 billion. Saskatchewan, a smaller economy, still contributes far more than it gets back. The equalization system is designed to keep Quebec politically pacified, but at what cost? Westerners grow weary of paying for a system that refuses to acknowledge their needs. Alberta's talk of a provincial pension plan, modelled after Quebec's withdrawal from the Canada Pension Plan, is not just political posturing. It is a stern warning that patience is running out.

In a way, Quebec is a tutor for Western discontent. Since the 1960s, it has been exploring its options, flexing its muscles, forcing the rest of Canada to accept that it had the right in principle to secede from the federation if it chose to. The referendums and the Clarity Act that followed the 1995 vote laid down the terms for provincial sovereignty: a clear majority voting in a referendum for succession, followed by negotiations with the federal and provincial governments. Those were the rules that would allow Quebec to leave. They are also the rules that would allow Alberta and/or Saskatchewan to leave.

While Alberta and Saskatchewan fight against federal interference, British Columbia presents a stark contrast. The province has embraced diversification, thriving in technology, tourism, and international trade. Vancouver has become more than ever Canada's gateway to the Pacific, with 40 per cent of its exports going to Asian markets, particularly China, Japan, and South Korea. British Columbia's demographic profile is also distinct. More than 30 per cent of its population is foreign-born, compared to 16 per cent in Alberta and 13 per cent in Saskatchewan and Manitoba. This diversity has shaped its politics and culture. Whereas Alberta and Saskatchewan lean conservative—notwithstanding Rachel Notley's tenure as NDP premier—British Columbia flirts with both sides of the political spectrum.

The environmental movement in British Columbia has real power, often placing the province at odds with Alberta's resource-driven economy. The battle over pipelines is only the most visible manifestation of this divide. For Alberta, pipelines are economic lifelines. For many in British Columbia, they are environmental vandalism. The Trans Mountain Pipeline expansion, which Alberta viewed as a necessity, faced years of opposition from British Columbia's government and environmental activists. This tension fractured any notion of absolute Western unity.

Manitoba remains politically and economically distinct from its Western neighbours. While agriculture remains a cornerstone of its economy, the province has a presence in finance, manufacturing, and hydroelectric power. Its politics are more centrist, reflecting a mix of rural conservatism and urban progressivism. Manitoba has the highest proportion of Indigenous residents of any province, making reconciliation and Indigenous economic inclusion central issues.

Despite their differences, the Western provinces experience common frustrations. The equalization system is outdated and unfair. Federal climate policies are crafted to appease urban voters in Central Canada while punishing resource-producing provinces. The political dominance of Ontario and Quebec has historically made Western concerns secondary in federal decision making.

This growing political divide is shaping the nation's future. The federal government can continue pretending Western grievances can be ignored, but the anger is not going away. The question is whether Canada's political establishment will finally take the Wests seriously or continue to gamble that Alberta and Saskatchewan's patience will never truly run out. That gamble would be risky in the extreme.

🍁

William Butler Yeats could have been thinking about Canada's growing regional crisis when he wrote "The Second Coming" in 1919. His oft-quoted line "Things fall apart; the centre cannot hold" feels less like poetry and more like prophecy.

Pierre Poilievre sought to build on the Big Shift that Stephen Harper forged during his decade in power. For a while, it looked as though the old Laurentian Consensus, with its stranglehold on power, had been shattered, as suburban Ontario voters joined the Conservative base of rural Ontario and the West. But Donald Trump's threat to Ontario's manufacturing base pushed suburban immigrant voters back into the Liberal tent.

The fault lines remain, however, as serious as ever. The PQ aims for winning conditions for a sovereignty referendum if it returns to government in Quebec City. At the same time, Alberta and Saskatchewan once again find themselves outside the Central Canadian consensus. Alberta might even hold a sovereignty referendum of its own. And hanging over everything is the Trump administration, now well into its second term. Its America First economic policies threaten the stability of the global economy, which destabilizes Canada as well.

For decades, the Laurentian elite believed that no matter how loud the West shouted, no matter how restless Quebec became, no matter how deep national divisions ran, Canada would always find a way to muddle through. But maybe those old assumptions no longer apply. Canada has survived on compromise, inertia, and a stubborn refusal to confront its contradictions. But in this new era, an era of rising Western defiance, polls favouring the Parti Québécois in Quebec, and economic warfare from an unpredictable White House, those old survival strategies may lead Canada to a breaking point.

FOUR

THE GENERATION GAP

Many young Canadians are giving up on their future. They might one day be prepared to give up on Canada itself. This is not hyperbole; this is data. An October 2023 poll by Nanos Research revealed that 70 per cent of Canadians—including 75 per cent of adults under thirty-five—believe the next generation will experience a lower standard of living compared to today. Young Canadians are poorer, more indebted, and more economically precarious than any generation in modern history. The social contract that promised each generation at least as good a life as the previous one is broken.

Central to the pessimism by and toward the young is home-ownership, or the lack of it. Owning a home, a cornerstone of middle-class aspiration since the end of the Second World War, was once within reach for the average Canadian family.

For decades, hard work and financial discipline were usually enough to secure a place of one's own. Not anymore. In 1976, the average price of a home in Canada was about $57,000, roughly three and a half times the median household income. Today, the benchmark home price has soared past $750,000, more than eight times the median income. In cities like Toronto and Vancouver, the gap is even more extreme, with price-to-income ratios exceeding ten to one.

In major cities, today, the average mortgage payment swallows more than 60 per cent of a household's income, according to a December 2023 report by RBC Economics. The mortgage payment as a percentage of income (MPPI) for non-condo properties in the Greater Toronto Area is now 81 per cent. That's right, Torontonians are now shelling out eight dollars of every ten they earn in pre-tax household income just to cover the mortgage for the average middle-class house in Canada's most populous city.

Young Canadians have responded by giving up on home-ownership. According to a June 2024 Ipsos poll, three quarters of Canadian adults under thirty-five believe that owning a home is now a privilege reserved for the rich. The home-buying numbers bear this out. According to the Bank of Canada, in 1981, 55 per cent of Canadians aged twenty-five to thirty-four owned a home. By 2024, that figure had plummeted to just 36 per cent, a stark reflection of how affordability has collapsed for many younger Canadians.

Young renters aren't catching a break either. In 2023, the average rent for a one-bedroom apartment in Toronto soared to $2,500 per month, marking a staggering 20 per cent increase in just one year, says rentals.ca. Although rents have come down a bit recently, the increasing cost of other essentials has clawed back any savings. Grocery costs surged by more than 11 per cent in 2022, the largest annual increase in four decades, and there is no sign of prices coming back down. And all this was before Donald Trump's tariffs kicked in.

The housing crisis is not the result of a failure of capitalism but of a failure to allow capitalism to function. Restrictive zoning laws, slow bureaucratic approvals, and excessive red tape have strangled housing supply, making it nearly impossible for developers to meet demand. In places like Texas, where fewer building restrictions exist, housing remains far more affordable despite strong population growth. Canada's political class has prioritized protecting existing homeowners over enabling new construction, leaving young Canadians with few options other than lifelong renting or moving elsewhere.

It's not just the cost of housing that is driving despair among the young. It's the fact that soaring home prices have not been offset by rising wages for younger Canadians. Their earnings have remained stagnant in real terms for decades. In 1985, according to Statistics Canada, the median after-tax income for a twenty-five- to thirty-four-year-old Canadian worker was approximately $51,000 in today's dollars. By 2022, that figure had inched up to just over $52,000. That's a mere 2 per cent increase over nearly forty years, barely keeping pace with inflation.

Higher education, once the golden ticket to middle-class stability for young Canadians, has turned into an expensive gamble. The average tuition for an undergraduate degree in Canada has more than tripled since the early 1990s. The average graduate now carries more than $28,000 in student debt, with many owing far more. And unlike previous generations, many of today's graduates are finding that their degrees do not guarantee stable, well-paying, middle-class jobs. Instead, they are bouncing between short-term contracts, part-time gigs, and side hustles just to make ends meet. According to a 2024 Harris survey, 87 per cent of Canadian job seekers have worked a side gig at some point in their careers, with 29 per cent currently maintaining a side gig during company hours. This trend is more pronounced among younger generations, with 41 per cent of Gen Z and 47 per cent of millennials indicating they would work a side gig on company time if they thought they could get away with it.

The combined impact of skyrocketing housing costs, stagnant wages, precarious employment, and the rising cost of higher education has left many young Canadians trapped in an extended adolescence. Unable to afford homes, they are delaying marriage and children while relying on financial support from their parents well into their thirties. Nearly 40 per cent of Canadians aged twenty to thirty-four still live with their parents—the highest proportion in modern history, according to Statistics Canada. In Toronto, that number jumps to 47 per cent, almost half. Similar trends are playing out across Canada's major cities, where an entire generation is being locked out of the financial independence that defined their parents' early adulthood.

As young Canadians struggle, their parents and grandparents are doing just fine. In the economic race between young and old, older Canadians are winning decisively, while younger Canadians are falling further behind. The financial divide between generations has never been wider, and the data proves it. If homeownership is an impossible hurdle for most young Canadians to overcome, for many older Canadians, it's a windfall. The average homeowner who bought in the 1980s or 1990s has seen their home value increase five or six times over. Many are mortgage-free and have hundreds of thousands, if not millions, of dollars in home equity.

The income gap tells a similar story. Whereas wages for younger Canadians have stagnated for decades, Canadian workers between fifty-five and sixty-four have seen their after-tax incomes rise by more than 30 per cent in real terms since 1985. Their wages have kept pace with inflation and then some. Their wealth has accumulated while younger generations scrape by, drowning in debt and struggling with a cost of living that has soared far beyond their earning power.

The retirement gap is just as stark. Many older Canadians are sitting on gold-plated pensions, benefiting from generous employer-sponsored plans that younger Canadians can only dream of. The percentage of workers covered by a defined benefit pension plan has plummeted from 46 per cent in the 1970s to just 22 per cent today, with most of those remaining plans held by government workers. For those without a pension, there is the Canada Pension Plan, Old Age Security, the Guaranteed Income Supplement for low-income seniors, and private savings. Older Canadians have had decades to accumulate wealth. The median net worth of Canadians aged sixty-five and older now exceeds $1 million, while Canadians under thirty-five have a median net worth of just $48,000.

Not only are young people locked out of homeownership and economic security, they are also expected to bear the financial burden of an aging population. Canada's fertility rate has

collapsed to 1.26, far below the replacement rate of 2.1, mean-
ing fewer workers will be responsible for supporting a growing
number of retirees. Today, there are roughly three working-age
Canadians for every senior. By 2040, that ratio is projected
to drop to two to one. The costs of health care, pensions, and
social services will skyrocket, all funded by a younger workforce already struggling to build financial stability.

Once a country falls into demographic decline, reversing
the trend becomes nearly impossible. Without decisive action,
Canada faces a future of declining living standards, shrinking economic influence, and deteriorating quality of life. The
numbers do not lie. If the birth rate continues to fall and young
people remain locked out of economic opportunity, Canada
will become smaller, poorer, and politically unstable. It will
be a nation defined by economic stagnation, intergenerational
conflict, and an aging population demanding ever greater support from an overburdened and shrinking workforce.

For now, Canada's economy is sustained by the spending
power of older generations who benefited from decades of
rising home prices, stable employment, and defined benefit
pensions. But this financial cushion will not last forever. As
boomers begin transferring their wealth, many younger Canadians will find little left to inherit. Rising long-term care costs,
reverse mortgages, and increasing tax burdens will erode much
of the financial security that older generations accumulated.
The long-promised intergenerational wealth transfer may be
more of a trickle than a flood.

This growing disparity is not just an economic issue. It is
a political crisis in the making. The concentration of wealth
among older Canadians is fuelling resentment and creating

the conditions for social unrest that could shake the foundations of Canadian society. If younger generations come to see Canada as a country that serves only the interests of older and wealthier homeowners, they may choose to dismantle the system rather than work within it. If they do not expect to inherit a social safety net for the elderly that their taxes support, they may vote for politicians who propose to scrap the net altogether.

For young Canadians already locked out of the housing market and struggling to build stable careers, immigration is another added pressure they cannot ignore. The promise of immigration has always been one of economic growth, innovation, and a stronger workforce. And for much of Canadian history, that promise held true. But today, millions of permanent residents, international students, temporary workers, and asylum seekers compete with younger Canadians for housing, wages, and public services. New arrivals push up housing costs and push down wages, with younger workers paying the price. A 2024 report from Statistics Canada showed that the labour force participation rate for immigrants is now higher than that of Canadian-born workers. The solution is not to shut the door on immigrants but to ensure that younger Canadians are not forced to compete with newcomers for a place to stay and for a living wage.

❦

For many young Canadians, the economic struggles of today are not just about money. They are about hope—or rather, the lack of it. The relentless combination of unaffordable housing, stagnant wages, rising costs, and a precarious job market takes a psychological toll. Anxiety and depression among young Canadians are at record highs, with mental health professionals pointing directly to financial instability and uncertainty about the future as driving factors. According to a 2024 survey by the Canadian Mental Health Association, more than 50 per cent of Canadians aged eighteen to thirty-four report feeling pessimistic about their financial future. The result is a generation that feels trapped—unable to see a viable path toward financial security and stability.

This despair manifests not only in personal anxiety but in a broader disengagement from national institutions and even national identity. Surveys report that between 20 and 30 per cent of young Canadians express strong national pride, compared to more than 60 per cent of those aged fifty-five and older. The declining faith in Canada's future is not hard to understand. When young people struggle to secure necessities, when they feel priced out of their own cities, when they see no realistic way to build a stable life in their own home, attachment to their country can only weaken.

The ethno-cultural composition of today's young Canadian population also contributes to the weakness of national attachment. Gone are the days when the typical Canadian youth was a churchgoing, hockey-playing descendant of European stock. Today, many young people found in the sprawling suburbs of major cities celebrate Diwali or the Lunar New Year, tracing their roots to continents other than Europe. Such diversity fuels cultural and economic innovation, but it can also make it harder for everyone to have a shared understanding of their society and a shared set of assumptions that anchor it.

Canada's ethnic diversity has reached levels that may never have been experienced by any country. The 2021 census revealed that nearly 27 per cent of Canadians identify as visible minorities, a figure that reaches 55 per cent in both greater Toronto and Vancouver, making the term "minority" meaningless. The younger members of these communities grow up as Canadians but also embrace global influences far beyond the European roots of previous generations. Cleavages emerge between the rural parts of the country, where the culture retains its white, Christian, European identity, and cosmopolitan cities in which many residents shop at a Tamil grocer, worship at a Sikh gurdwara, or send their child to a Mandarin immersion school.

Religious affiliation among young Canadians is also changing at an unprecedented pace. While most Canadians once considered themselves Christians, at least culturally—showing up for church at Christmas and Easter; getting married there; having their babies baptized—the 2021 census showed that 35 per cent of Canadians now report no religious affiliation at all, even as the number of people identifying with Islam, Hinduism, Sikhism, and Buddhism grows rapidly, particularly among younger generations.

Unlike their parents and grandparents, who often maintained rigid cultural distinctions, today's youth fluidly blend influences from multiple backgrounds. They listen to K-pop, watch Bollywood films, mix English or French with their parents' native tongue, think nothing of eating sushi at lunch and grabbing a shawarma after work. More than 450 ethnic or cultural origins were reported in the last census, a staggering reflection of just how complex Canadian identity has become.

As immigration reshapes Canada's demographics, it is also redefining the country's political, economic, and cultural future. A nation built by French and English and Irish, by Germans and Ukrainians and Italians and Greeks, by settlers scattered in farms and towns and cities across a vast, cold landscape, is now submerged in a dense, urban matrix of multicultures. Societies with cultural, religious, and linguistic differences risk civic unrest unless they are able to master a shared national purpose. While Canada embraced its multicultural mosaic, the United States insisted that newcomers embrace the American Way, whatever that way might be. Other societies, such as Japan or South Korea, have preserved distinctive national identities by largely excluding newcomers.

The challenge facing Canada in the third decade of the twenty-first century is not whether it can continue to grow through immigration, but whether it can project a sense of national self that all newcomers can understand and embrace— a national identity in which both they and native-born citizens see themselves as part of the same future. If that effort fails, fragmentation and resentment will follow.

This challenge is not only cultural but economic. If the next generation, regardless of its cultural heritage, does not see Canada as a place of opportunity, it will disengage, not just from the economy but from civic life, politics, and the very idea of Canada itself. If nothing changes, the country risks losing more than just economic productivity. It risks losing the trust and investment of its own future.

✿

The crisis of confidence and faith in the future among younger voters has led to a tectonic political shift that few analysts saw coming: the shift of young voters to the right. For generations, young voters in Canada and across the Western world have been a reliable constituency for progressive parties. But that pattern is changing. Throughout the West, from Sweden to France to the United States, young men in particular are increasingly turning to right-wing and populist politics. The same trend is emerging in Canada. In the 2025 election, according to Nanos, 50 per cent of voters under thirty-five supported the Conservative Party.

This is not the first time young people have turned to conservative politicians. In the late 1970s and early 1980s, economic stagnation and growing frustration with government overreach led to a generational realignment. Young voters who had once favoured left-leaning policies turned to conservative leaders such as Ronald Reagan, Margaret Thatcher, and Brian Mulroney, who championed economic growth, personal responsibility, and a reduced role for government in daily life. The political preferences of younger Canadians today appear to be moving in a similar direction, particularly among young men who feel the status quo has failed them.

While economic frustration is a major driver of this shift, another key factor is the changing perception of the left. Once the champion of the working class and youth, progressive parties are now widely seen as part of the political establishment. Young men struggling to build their futures see little tangible action from traditional left-leaning parties to address their concerns.

Beyond economic grievances, a broader sense of anti-elitism drives this shift. Populist rhetoric that challenges government bureaucracy, cultural institutions, and academia resonates with those who feel ignored by political and cultural elites. This growing discontent is further amplified by cultural backlash. Many young men perceive progressive social policies as exclusionary or overly focused on identity. They resent narratives that cast them as privileged when in fact they are struggling and insecure.

A crisis of masculinity has further deepened this divide. In a world that increasingly emphasizes gender equity, diversity, and social inclusion, some young men feel adrift. Figures such as the Canadian psychologist Jordan Peterson, who push back against modern feminism and social-justice movements, have gained traction among disaffected young men. For some, this has led to increased support for right-wing movements that promise to restore a sense of purpose and stability in a rapidly changing cultural landscape.

Young Canadian men really are falling behind, compared not only to young Canadian women but also to previous generations of men. In education, the job market, and mental well-being, young men in Canada struggle in ways that would have been unimaginable a generation ago. The data paints a grim picture for men. As of 2021, 70 per cent of Canadian women aged twenty-five to sixty-four held a postsecondary degree or diploma, compared to just 64 per cent of men. Among younger adults aged twenty-five to thirty-four, the gap was even more pronounced: 76 per cent of women had completed postsecondary education, while only 66 per cent of men had done the same. It's true that a postsecondary degree isn't what it used to be, but it remains the most reliable path to better employment opportunities and higher earnings. Yet young men are increasingly shutting themselves out of both.

As more women graduate with advanced credentials, they are moving into high paying, stable jobs, while men are over-represented in fields that are shrinking or becoming more precarious. The employment rate for university graduates in Canada stands at 74 per cent, compared to just 55 per cent for those with only a high school diploma. As automation and economic shifts continue to devalue traditionally male-dominated trades and manufacturing jobs, the divide is widening. A May 2025 Statistics Canada report found that, for the first time ever, more young men than women in Canada are not in education, employment, or training (NEET). This is transformational. For millennia, men assumed that they were the breadwinners, that women belonged in the home rais-ing the family. For generations, women struggled for property rights, then voting rights, then reproductive rights, then the right to equal employment. Not every gap has closed, but the fact that women are now more present in the workforce than men marks an epic shift. And although many men celebrate these gains with women, some men resent their loss of status, even as the reliable blue-collar work that allowed many of their fathers to own a home, and maybe even a small boat or RV, disappears, replaced by the knowledge economy.

The more that young men feel shut out of traditional paths to success, the more they become susceptible to populist and reactionary movements. The appeal is clear. A generation of men who feel left behind is looking for someone to blame. Internationally, media figures like Joe Rogan have built massive followings by challenging progressive orthodoxy and voicing the frustrations of young men who feel abandoned by main-stream institutions. Social media is awash with influencers who tell young men that the system is rigged against them, and many are listening.

Beneath the economic and political frustrations lies another, more troubling reality. Young men are lonelier, more depressed, and more likely to die by suicide than their female counter-parts. Yet they are also far less likely to seek help. During the COVID-19 pandemic, 27 per cent of Canadian men reported worsening mental health, yet only 49 per cent of those sought assistance. The cultural script that tells men to be stoic and self-sufficient is proving deadly.

Canada's shifting economic and educational landscape has produced clear winners and losers, and young men are increasingly on the wrong side of that equation. Without intervention—such as educational policies that engage boys earlier, economic policies that create viable pathways for non-university graduates, and mental health initiatives tailored to men—this problem will only get worse. A generation of men without clear prospects is not just a demographic challenge. It is a social and political time bomb. If Canada wants a stable future, it cannot afford to leave its young men behind.

The youth crisis is not just a generational problem; it is a national one. Economic stagnation among young Canadians threatens long-term growth. If an entire generation is unable to accumulate wealth, the country's economic future will suf-fer. Social fragmentation is another risk. The growing divide between young men and women in political beliefs and eco-nomic prospects could fuel generational resentment and even unrest. And politically, trust in democracy is eroding. The rise of populist movements signals a loss of faith in traditional parties and institutions, a warning sign for Canada's stability.

In January 2025, as Donald Trump rattled his annexationist sabre, Ipsos asked Canadians whether they would vote for Canada to become part of the United States. Eight in ten said "never." But four in ten people under the age of thirty-five agreed with the statement that they would be willing to become citizens of the United States if they were offered "full citizenship, and a full conversion of the Canadian dollar and all personal financial assets into U.S. dollars."[1] That is how little attachment many of the younger generation feel toward Canada.

If governments continue to ignore these warning signs, the consequences will be dire. A generation that sees no future in Canada will either leave or turn against the system entirely. We have already seen political upheaval in other countries where young people, especially young men, feel abandoned by their leaders. In France, mass protests over economic inequality have shaken the foundations of government. In the United States, the collapse of faith in institutions has fuelled the rise of populist movements on both the left and the right. Canada is not immune. If young people believe the system is rigged against them, they will seek radical alternatives.

The economist Albert O. Hirschman identified three ways in which individuals respond to dissatisfaction: exit, voice, and loyalty. Exit is the most extreme response, occurring when people leave a job, abandon a brand, or end a failing marriage. Voice involves expressing concerns and advocating for change, whether through protests, negotiations, or reform efforts. Loyalty keeps individuals committed despite their frustrations, often delaying exit and encouraging voice as a means of improvement. Discussions about the crisis facing young people largely assume their loyalty, with some demanding voice. But what if exit becomes the more attractive option?

Exit is not a myth or a distant threat; it is already happening. The numbers tell the story. Since the pandemic ended, more than a hundred thousand people have left Canada permanently each year in search of better opportunities abroad. More are leaving each year than left the year before. Many are young, highly educated professionals who see little future in Canada's high-cost, low-opportunity economy. If this trend continues, the country risks losing its most promising talent. What happens when the most productive members of society decide they are better off elsewhere?

As for those young Canadians who stay, if they no longer see a future in this country, they will stop investing in it. They will not buy homes. They will not start businesses. They will not build families. A nation where an entire generation disengages is a nation in decline. By the time the political class takes notice, it may be too late, but this crisis did not emerge overnight. For years, successive Canadian governments ignored clear warning signs, failing to act on housing affordability, wage stagnation, and economic opportunity. The result has been a slow but relentless erosion of economic mobility.

This erosion is not the product of an unrestrained free market but rather of excessive government intervention. Well-intentioned but restrictive zoning laws have choked housing supply, sending prices skyrocketing. Burdensome credentialling requirements have blocked young people from entering skilled trades even as labour shortages worsen. High taxation and excessive regulation have stifled business investment, limiting the creation of stable, well-paying jobs. If government policies helped create this crisis, the solution is not more bureaucracy but the removal of barriers that prevent economic growth and opportunity.

This failure is not partisan; it is systemic. Both progressive and conservative governments at all levels have sidestepped these issues, prioritizing short-term political calculations over long-term generational stability. The message to young Canadians has been clear and consistent. Their struggles are not a priority. But a political realignment is coming. As young people recognize that the existing parties have little interest in addressing their concerns, new movements will emerge. Whether driven by the populist right, the radical left, or something entirely different, change is inevitable. Political leaders who fail to grasp this reality do so at their peril. If they refuse to act, they will soon face a reckoning from a generation with nothing left to lose.

FIVE

OUT OF PRINT

Most young people have never seen a newspaper. Oh, they may have picked up a print copy of the *Vancouver Sun* or the *Hamilton Spectator* or the *Fredericton Daily Gleaner*. But those wispy rags aren't real newspapers, the kind that dominated print journalism from the late 1800s until the early 2000s. Up until about twenty years ago, real newspapers would land each morning with a great thump at the front door—five or six sections on a Saturday, a kilogram in weight and thick as a phone book. But then, most young people have never seen a phone book.

Broadcast journalism is also a wraith of its former self. *The National*, the CBC's flagship news broadcast, drew a million viewers, on average, in the 1990s. Today, the number is below three hundred thousand, even though the Canadian population has grown from twenty-five million then to forty-one million now. A generation ago, most big radio stations had a newsroom. Today, those newsrooms are extinct.

For the legacy media, or the mainstream media, or whatever you want to call them, the situation is dire. According to government figures, more than 450 news outlets in Canada have closed since 2008. In the last five years alone, the Canadian Media Guild reports, ten thousand jobs in journalism disappeared. Many universities and colleges, including Western University, the University of Regina, Humber College, and Loyalist College, have shut down or suspended their journalism programs.

Let's take the *Ottawa Citizen* as an example. At its peak in the late 1980s, when John Ibbitson arrived there as a cub reporter, the *Citizen* had just under two hundred people in its newsroom. Reporters covered local news, business news, and sports. There was a movie critic and a drama critic, a team of editorial writers and an editorial cartoonist. The *Citizen* had bureaus on Parliament Hill, at Queen's Park, and in Brockville, Cornwall, and Pembroke.

The paper broke major stories, revealing scandals and controversies that led a federal defence minister to resign after being seen at a strip club, the city's mayor to resign over a conflict of interest, police to lay criminal charges against a senator for misusing public funds, and officials to resign after an investigation into mismanagement at the local Humane Society. During the First Gulf War, the *Citizen* had a reporter stationed in Dubai, reporting on Canada's military contribution to expelling Saddam Hussein from Iraq.

Today, the physical newsroom no longer exists. About thirty reporters, editors, and managers put out a print edition of about a dozen pages and an online edition that typically includes only a few stories by *Citizen* journalists, with freelance contributions, wire copy, and rewritten press releases accounting for the rest. There are other digital sites looking at Ottawa events, doing restaurant reviews, even reporting on City Hall now and then. But the major investigations that the *Citizen* once undertook are no more. During construction of the city's new light rail transit system, which opened in 2019, people in the know heard rumours about problems with construction and testing. In the old days, the *Citizen* would have acted on those rumours, appointing a team of journalists who might well have delivered scoops on problems plaguing the new rails and trains. Instead, the rumours went unexplored. When the LRT finally launched, the system suffered so many closures and delays that automobile traffic in Ottawa actually increased, as former transit users gave up on the problem-plagued service and started driving in to work.

❧

Some critics blame media concentration, vulture capitalists, or a lack of government support—or at least the wrong kind of support—for the crisis in journalism. There is some truth in all of those charges. But the real reason for the decline of news media in Canada and elsewhere was the inability of the companies that owned print and broadcast outlets to understand the internet.

When people started using the World Wide Web on their home computers in the mid-1990s, newspaper owners quickly realized the potential for online news. They also knew that their largest source of revenue, advertising, would be harder to pull in online than in print because there were so many competing websites. Most owners decided to seek market share first and worry about monetization later. Big mistake. Internet users quickly became used to the notion that news on the web would always be available for free. That assumption, once entrenched, proved almost impossible to dislodge.

The largest source of advertising revenue for most newspapers was the classified ad. A typical newspaper would include pages of them each day: brief notices notifying readers of apartments for rent, job postings, obituaries, and the like. It was the classifieds, even more than the full-page ads from Toyota or Eaton's—another relic of the past—that made newspapers profitable. But in 2000, Craig Newmark started to expand his new online classified advertising service into select American cities. Within a few years, Craigslist had spread across the United States and Canada. Classified ads in newspapers vanished almost literally overnight.

In the early 2000s, great American daily newspapers—the *Philadelphia Inquirer*, the *Miami Herald*, the *Chicago Tribune*, the *Los Angeles Times*—fell into crisis. Thousands of reporters and editors lost their jobs. Bureaus closed in Washington and overseas. Investigative reporting evaporated. Even covering city hall became difficult. In Canada, the layoffs arrived a few years later.

Major national publications in the United States and Canada—the *New York Times*, the *Wall Street Journal*, the

Globe and Mail, the *Financial Times*—did not rely on classifieds and stayed healthy for a few years. But then, in 2008, the smartphone arrived. People now relied on their iPhone or Galaxy to surf the web and social media for the news, which they still expected to read for free. Even worse, Facebook and Google could identify which users were searching for which products in ways that legacy publications could not. By 2020, Google and Facebook controlled more than 80 per cent of the advertising market. Newspapers were in crisis. Today, most are in their death throes.

A few members of what used to be called the mainstream media found a way to survive and even thrive. They generally had several things in common. Their owners did not panic and sell off the property as soon as times got tough. They realized that digital subscriptions would have to replace advertising, and threw up paywalls. And they had a well-educated and affluent readership. The *Globe* is not the only survivor among the legacy media in Canada. The *Winnipeg Free Press* continues to do excellent work and is rewarded by a loyal audience. *La Presse* has been successful since the Desmarais family turned it into a non-profit, took over its existing pension obligations, and bid it farewell. There are other examples to be found here and there.

But most metro daily newspapers are not able to generate enough subscriber interest and revenue to pay their way. It didn't help—in fact, it was a crucial reason for the crisis— that as revenues declined, family-owned businesses sold their papers to hedge funds that strip-mined the papers' assets. As ad revenue declined, managers laid off reporters and editors. Inevitably, quality declined. Revenues further declined. More layoffs. A vicious cycle.

There are alternatives. The *Tyee* is one site—and there are numerous others—that offers intelligent analysis of and opinion about political events from the left. The *Hub* does the same from the right. The *Narwhal* worked with the *Toronto Star* to break the story of Ontario premier Doug Ford's government's plans to sell Greenbelt lands to developers it favoured. Most communities now have a digital site that offers the latest news. But they are staffed by a handful of journalists rather than the dozens, or even hundreds, who once worked in the newsrooms of their print predecessors.

Think of it this way: In 2016, the *Guelph Mercury* closed. There is no CBC or CTV or Global station in this Ontario city west of Greater Toronto. There is local radio and a *Mercury* website, though it's largely devoid of news, and another digital site named *Guelph Today*. But there is nothing in the city that boasts even a fraction of the reporting power the *Mercury* had in its heyday. How can Guelph residents know what is going on at city hall? At the police department? At the University of Guelph?

Or think of it another way: Who will cover Canada's next major war? In 2005, Liberal prime minister Paul Martin committed Canada to supporting the NATO mission in Afghanistan. In 2006, his Conservative successor, Stephen Harper, affirmed that support. From then until the combat mission ended in 2011, major Canadian news organizations sent reporters to Kandahar, where the Canadian contingent was centred. Journalists paid a high price for covering the war. Michelle Lang of the *Calgary Herald* was killed by an exploding IED. Kathleen Kenna of the *Toronto Star* was gravely wounded in a separate incident. Two reporters were kidnapped and held for months before negotiations secured their release. Yet in newsrooms across the country, reporters continued to volunteer for an assignment whose greatest financial cost for many news organizations was life insurance.

The *Globe* is the only Canadian newspaper left with foreign correspondents and bureaus around the world. The CBC has foreign correspondents as well. Apart from relying on them, how will Canadians learn about the next event that sends the nation's troops into harm's way? Will we simply have to trust the press releases? The *Globe* remains the linchpin for print journalism in Canada. During the Afghanistan mission, its journalists uncovered evidence that Canadian troops were handing Taliban prisoners of war over to Afghan officials knowing the prisoners would be tortured. In more recent years, its reporters have uncovered everything from systemic police reluctance to investigate sexual assault allegations, to Justin Trudeau pressuring his attorney general to secure a plea agreement for a Quebec engineering firm. The *Globe* also revealed government waste and misspending during the pandemic, the abuse of a program that favoured Indigenous businesses, efforts by the Chinese government to influence federal elections, and much else.

But what did the *Globe* miss? In the past, the *Toronto Star* and the Southam (now Postmedia) papers had their fair share of scoops. The CBC was formidable, as were CTV and Global TV. All of them have fewer resources than in the past. Rarely do they announce the results of major investigations revealing incompetence or corruption. The decline of the major media in Canada mirrors and reinforces the decline of the Laurentian elite. Their world view dominated the editorial outlook of the major Central Canadian dailies. The Laurentian bias of the CBC is so grimly entrenched that Conservatives applauded Pierre Poilievre's vow to defund the English-language arm of the broadcaster if elected.

Meanwhile, readers turn to podcasts, Substack, and other alternative media to find out what's going on and what they should think about it. The Canadian political class and the surviving members of the Canadian media tend to sniff at these alternative sites, yet they exert a greater influence on politics and policy than their legacy counterparts. Substack offerings in Canada range from deeply respectable commentary—by such former legacy media columnists as Paul Wells and the writers at the Line, including Matt Gurney and Jen Gerson—to outrageous offerings on the left and right. And then there are podcasts, social media, and other online offerings.

Joe Rogan has 14.5 million followers on Spotify, plus however many listen to him on other platforms. An estimated eleven million people tune in to his podcast daily, making it one of the most popular offerings of that format in the United States and in the world. That audience skews toward younger males, and it skews conservative. Rogan himself isn't necessarily conservative—he supported same-sex marriage, universal public health care, and legal recreational drug use, for example—but in 2024 he endorsed Donald Trump, after hosting the Republican candidate for a podcast that earned forty-eight million views on YouTube. Democratic presidential candidate Kamala Harris turned down Rogan's invitation, preferring to show up on *Saturday Night Live* instead. *SNL* is beloved (if not often watched) by All the Best People, but not by the people who decide elections. Following the election,

Variety magazine declared Rogan "the most powerful person in media by far."[1] (He has competition, though, from a new, anti-Trump network, MeidasTouch.)

Rogan is powerful because he speaks to the manosphere, to the "bro" vote. These young men are often blue collar, with relatively little education but great resentment that society no longer treats them as the alpha males they long to be. Although most of them are white, and some are white nationalist, others are Black or Latino. Trump did surprisingly well among those voters as well. The bro vote also includes tech lords and venture capitalists from Silicon Valley who feel excluded from coastal elites, too, and who have the money and power to influence the vote. Elon Musk was the most visible among their ranks, both before and after the election, but those ranks also included inventors and investors Peter Thiel, Marc Andreessen, and Ben Horowitz.

Although such figures exert less influence in Canadian politics—venture capital firms being rare here, and campaign donation limits strict—modern conservatism both seeks the bro vote and inhabits the media they inhabit. Pierre Poilievre turned down an invitation to appear on Rogan's show, which may have been a mistake, but he did offer an extended interview to Jordan Peterson, who also has a huge following in the manosphere.

During their nine-plus years in power, the Liberals did everything they could to preserve the legacy media, demonstrating in the process the law of unintended consequences working to savage effect. As newspaper owners pleaded for help, the government initially came up with about $100 million a year in direct and indirect financial support, including everything from tax credits for subscriptions to payroll subsidies. These subsidies were a bad idea for several reasons: First, they only allowed legacy publications to survive at the barebones level they had deteriorated into; second, any profits from them tended to flow to the foreign hedge funds that owned these companies; third, they eroded public trust in the media. After all, the government they were supposed to be scrutinizing was keeping them afloat.

The Liberals' biggest gamble came in the form of the Online News Act, which was premised on the dubious notion that Google and Facebook robbed news media of revenue while profiting by posting links to news stories from those sites. In reality, the news media were keen to have their links presented by those sites, because readers who clicked would see advertising as well as editorial content from the legacy site. Nonetheless, the new act required Facebook and Google to pay into a fund that would be used to further prop up the old newspapers. Upon passage of the bill, parent company Meta simply removed Canadian news links from Facebook and Instagram. Not only was there no new money, but news organizations lost an important source of online readership. Companies that already had agreements with Facebook saw those agreements cancelled. New start-ups that depended on Facebook to get their name and stories out to readers lost that opportunity as well. Though Google ultimately agreed to throw $100 million into the pot annually, the Online News Act damaged more than helped the industry.

We confront an unsettled landscape. The traditional media, whether it be the metro daily newspaper, the top-of-the-hour radio newscast, or the evening news at 10 or 11 p.m., continue to lose readers and viewers, with only a few legacy publications able to attract the loyalty and credit cards of subscribers. New media inhabit a fractured landscape of both real and alternative facts, sometimes informing but often simply catering to and inflaming the passions of their audience.

This is what we should fear: People with enough education and knowledge will understand the importance of having access to hard facts, informed analysis, and intelligent opinion. They will pay the hundreds of dollars a year it costs to subscribe to the *Globe and Mail* or the *New York Times* or *Bloomberg News* or the *Economist*. Everyone else will rely on their social media feeds, which will stoke their passions and inflame their prejudices. In such an environment, how do you preserve a healthy democracy? In the United States, this has become an urgent, frightening question.

There is reason to hope: that the best of the legacy media will grow and prosper, that new formats will emerge as technology evolves, that when Canada next goes to war there will be journalists to cover it—though how they cover it may be as unfamiliar to us today as a modern drone would have been to a soldier in past wars.

The non-profit sector might come to the rescue. There might or might not be a role for government. We can only hope. Because the news media don't just keep us informed. They also help reinforce Canada's identity—or at least identities—as a nation. They tell us who we are. And as a PBS documentary asked more than fifteen years ago: Without newspapers, what will we know?

SIX

CANADA ALONE

Foreign policy is defence policy. The one determines the other. Canada's foreign policy today lies in a shambles in part because Canada's defences have never been so weak. The long downhill slide began with the scrapping of the *Bonnie*.

It will surprise many Canadians to hear that the Canadian navy once included aircraft carriers. Canadians manned two Royal Navy carriers during the Second World War. At the end of that war, this country had the world's third-largest navy, the kind of navy that considered it right and proper to have a carrier as part of its fleet.

The light fleet carrier *Warrior*, built for Canada by the British, entered service in 1946, but it proved unsuitable for Canadian winters and was replaced in 1948 by the *Magnificent*, which spent much of the next decade travelling the world on

CANADA ALONE   87

training cruises and participating in NATO fleet exercises. One of *Maggie's* last major missions was to transport a force of Canadian peacekeepers—the first of their kind—to uphold the agreement that ended the Suez Crisis of 1956, for which Lester Pearson, then external affairs minister, received the Nobel Peace Prize.

The *Magnificent* was replaced in 1957 by the larger and more modern *Bonaventure*, with its complement of Banshee fighter jets and Tracker antisubmarine aircraft. The *Bonnie*, as it was affectionately known, and its destroyer escorts specialized in antisubmarine warfare. Darrell Bricker remembers as a child gazing at the imposing mass of the vessel going under the Angus L. Macdonald Bridge as his parents drove him from Dartmouth to Halifax.

In 1968, just after the *Bonnie* had undergone a midlife refit, the newly elected Liberal government headed by Prime Minister Pierre Trudeau ordered a defence review. Trudeau thought that Canada had become too much of an appendage of the United States; he wanted to adopt a more independent, even neutral, foreign policy. Perversely, his cabinet concluded that greater independence could best be achieved by weakening, rather than strengthening, Canada's defences. But the real purpose of the review was to divert spending from the military to social programs. Following completion of the review, the Trudeau government cut Canada's contribution to NATO in Europe by 50 per cent and decommissioned the *Bonaventure*. The military's trajectory has been downhill ever since.

Today, Canada is the worst laggard in NATO, the only major military member that spends less than 2 per cent of its GDP on defence even as Russian troops occupy parts of Ukraine and threaten our NATO allies, and as both the Russians and the Chinese test our sovereignty in the Arctic. Worse still, the United States, for so long the umbrella that protected Canada, now questions our very right to exist.

We are alone in the world. And we have only ourselves to blame.

❋

Canada has a proud military tradition. During the War of 1812, British regulars and Canadian militia, alongside Indigenous allies, repelled repeated American invasions. A recently added monument on Parliament Hill commemorating that war includes soil from ten battle sites where Canadians fought for freedom. During the First World War, the Germans came to fear the Canadian Corps above all others. In the Second World War, on D-Day, June 6, 1944, five divisions landed on the beaches of Normandy: three American, two British, and one Canadian. And Canada sent two brigades to bolster United Nations forces during the Korean War.

In 1964, at the request of U.S. president Lyndon Johnson, Canada agreed to send peacekeeping troops to Cyprus, where civil strife threatened to escalate into war between Greece and Turkey. "You'll never know what this may have prevented," Johnson told Lester Pearson. "Now what can I do for you?" As Pearson observed in his memoirs, "I had some credit in the bank."[1] The next year, Canada and the United States agreed to the Auto Pact, which guaranteed that as many automobiles would be made in Canada as were sold in Canada. That agreement launched the integrated North American automobile industry. "I believe that Johnson's willingness to agree to the Auto Pact the next year, an agreement that hugely benefited Canada's auto sector, may well have been Pearson's reward for Cyprus,"wrote historian J.L. Granatstein years later.[2]

Lyndon Johnson asked Lester Pearson to send a peace-keeping force to Cyprus because the American president knew Canada was up to the job. The country was able to swiftly dispatch a battalion-sized force that could be supported both by air and by sea. The *Bonaventure* was crucial to the support. But this was exactly the sort of ready-aye-ready response that convinced Trudeau that Canadians were spending far too much contributing to America's defence needs. Trudeau soon discovered, though, that cutting defence spending and weakening alliance commitments came with a price. When, as part of the government's "third option" strategy of diversifying trade, the prime minister sought to forge closer trading ties with Europe, West German chancellor Helmut Schmidt reportedly told him, "No tanks, no trade."[3] The Liberal government increased its defence budget from 1.7 per cent of GDP in 1979 to 2.1 per cent in 1984. It also arranged to purchase West German Leopard tanks. Foreign policy is defence policy is trade policy.

Brian Mulroney knew on what side the bread was buttered. He kept defence spending at 2 per cent of GDP through most of his decade in office, despite cutting spending elsewhere to reduce the deficit. He was a stalwart supporter of Ronald Reagan's successful effort to end the Cold War by winning it. As Soviet influence in Eastern Europe crumbled, the major powers agreed on the terms of German reunification in 1990 during the Open Skies conference in Ottawa. And during these fateful events, Canada and the United States signed their historic free trade agreement in January 1988.

But Jean Chrétien and his finance minister, Paul Martin, were determined to bring the federal budget into balance. And with the Cold War over and the Soviet Union dismantled, governments across NATO were cashing in on the so-called peace dividend. By 2000, defence spending had fallen to about 1 per cent of GDP in Canada. Coupled with a scandal involving the torture and murder of a Somali teenager during a peacekeeping mission, this pushed the Canadian military to a nadir of reputation and combat readiness.

When he took office in 2006, Stephen Harper had grand dreams for the Canadian Forces. Along with restoring the individual identity of the three services, the Conservatives promised to increase troop strength, establish a heavy-lift capability at CFB Trenton, construct a deep-water port in the Arctic, and acquire three heavy icebreakers capable of carrying troops. But apart from the acquisition of five Boeing CC-177 Globemaster heavy-lift aircraft, few of the Tory dreams came true. Equipping the troops in Kandahar with tanks, helicopters, and other equipment diverted funds meant for other purposes, and the financial crisis of 2008–09 forced spending into non-defence-related areas. The icebreakers were downgraded to offshore patrol vessels, the Arctic port became a summertime refuelling station, long-promised helicopters never arrived, and the on-again, off-again acquisition of Lockheed Martin F-35 fighter jets turned into a national embarrassment.

By the time the Conservatives left office in 2015, defence spending once again hovered around 1 per cent of GDP.

"The failure to learn from history ended up dooming Harper's vision for national defence," Queen's University political scientist Kim Richard Nossal concluded in his damning assessment of the Conservatives' defence failures.[4] Harper could never square the need to spend large sums on defence with the general reluctance among Canadians to do so. In 2014, responding to Russia's illegal annexation of Crimea, NATO members committed to spending 2 per cent of GDP on defence. Harper signed on behalf of Canada. But like most member states, this country then ignored the pledge.

Canada's global reputation continued to slide under Harper's watch, too. In 2010, the country failed in its attempt at securing a temporary seat on the UN Security Council, the first time Canada had been unable to garner enough votes to win. (We lost out to Germany and Portugal.)

After Justin Trudeau defeated Stephen Harper in 2015, the new prime minister declared "Canada is back" on the world stage. And initially people believed him. When Trudeau visited the Lester B. Pearson Building, headquarters to the foreign affairs department, workers came out of their offices to applaud him. The cool new Canadian prime minister received rave headlines and reviews in the international press. And at first, he was as good as his word. To fulfill the pledge that Canada would airlift thousands of Syrian refugees, public servants cancelled holidays, worked Christmas week, and volunteered to come over from other departments to lend a hand. Trudeau greeted the first planeload at Toronto's airport with new winter coats. "Welcome home," he told them. It was a moving moment for all Canadians. Progressive Americans contrasted Trudeau's actions with Donald Trump's brutal, racist efforts to deport undocumented immigrants and limit travel from Muslim countries. "Is he the free world's best hope?" *Rolling Stone* asked in June 2017.[5]

And as we've seen, the Trudeau government acted decisively to conclude trade agreements with European and Pacific nations, and with the United States. But then everything went south. The first big mess involved those Pacific trade talks. After Donald Trump withdrew the United States from the Trans-Pacific Partnership, the remaining eleven nations resolved to press ahead. The heads of government were ready to endorse the accord at a meeting of the Asia-Pacific Economic Cooperation forum in Da Nang, Vietnam, in November 2017. But Trudeau failed to show up for the meeting, and Canada sent word it wasn't ready to sign. The snub infuriated the Japanese, who had been leading the talks. The Australians were just as angry. Eventually, all sides agreed to new wording that included cultural protections Canada was insisting on. The leaders signed the renamed Comprehensive and Progressive Agreement for Trans-Pacific Partnership in Santiago, Chile, in March 2018. But Trudeau's classless performance in Da Nang left a bad taste in the mouths of other leaders.

Resentment morphed into ridicule when Trudeau, his wife Sophie Grégoire Trudeau, and their children visited India in February 2018. The Indians were bemused by the colourful costumes the Trudeaus traipsed around in, and Indian commentators openly mocked the Bollywood attire. "Too Indian, even for an Indian," *Outlook India* magazine concluded.[6] And the Indian government was enraged to discover that the Canadian contingent included Jaspal Atwal, a member of an extremist Sikh organization who had been convicted in Canada of the attempted assassination of a visiting Indian state cabinet minister. The *Washington Post* dubbed the trip "a total disaster."[7]

But the fiasco in India was small potatoes compared to the crisis in relations with China. Initially, Trudeau had hoped to improve those relations. His fondness for the regime in Beijing ran in his genes. The Canadian government led by his father Pierre had famously recognized Mao's China a full year before the United States. The Liberals under Jean Chrétien had embarked on the first Team Canada mission to deepen trade and investment ties with the Middle Kingdom in 1994. Justin had infamously remarked in 2013, "There's a level of admiration I actually have for China. Their basic dictatorship is actually allowing them to turn their economy around on a dime."[8] Many wondered at him expressing public admiration for a regime that prohibited free speech and imprisoned critics. In fairness, Xi Jinping had only come to power the year before and there was no general awareness of his intent to suppress democratic activity in Hong Kong or to fiercely persecute the Uyghurs and other Turkic minorities. In principle, and even in practice, a free trade agreement with China would have been a welcome step toward the goal of trade diversification.

But that all came a cropper during Trudeau's 2017 visit to Beijing, which was supposed to end with an announcement that trade talks had commenced. The Chinese scuttled the talks when it became clear that Canada would demand language on environmental protection and support for the rights of women and labour. Relations with China were worse at the end of 2017 than they were when the Liberals took office.

Worse went to worst in 2018, when Canadian officials detained Huawei executive Meng Wanzhou while she was changing planes at Vancouver International Airport. The Americans had charged the Huawei executive with violating U.S. sanctions against Iran and they wanted her extradited. Meng was the daughter of Huawei's founder, Ren Zhengfei, and the Chinese government went ballistic, imposing sanctions on Canadian agricultural exports and detaining two innocent Canadian civilians, Michael Kovrig and Michael Spavor. John Manley, who had been a senior minister in the Chrétien governments, thought it was a mistake for the Canadians to honour the Americans' request. "It was a good opportunity for a little bit of creative incompetence on the part of Canadian authorities and somehow just miss her," he told CBC.[9] In retrospect, he was probably right. The affair dragged on for almost three years, until President Joe Biden's administration agreed to a deferred prosecution, which led to the release of both Meng and the two Michaels.

Many Liberals had criticized Stephen Harper for supporting Taiwan and for refusing to attend the Beijing Olympics. Protecting business interests compelled him to adopt a more conciliatory approach to China. But relations between Ottawa and Beijing were far worse at the end of nine years of Justin Trudeau than they ever were during Stephen Harper's tenure.

By the time Trudeau began his third government in 2021, Canada was anything but back. The country had once again lost its bid for a seat on the Security Council. Infinitely worse, it had abandoned Afghan translators and others who had assisted the Canadian mission when the United States withdrew from Afghanistan as the Taliban regained control. The government offered strong support for Ukraine after the Russians wantonly invaded that country in February 2022, and Canada accepted more than three hundred thousand refugees fleeing the war. But the Trudeau government refused to join other NATO members in increasing defence spending. That decision was unconscionable. "With his invasion of Ukraine on Thursday, President Putin created a new reality," German chancellor Olaf Scholz told the Bundestag. "This reality demands a clear response. We have given it."[10] Germany, once as much a laggard in defence spending as Canada, moved swiftly to meet its 2 per cent commitment. So did other former low spenders, such as Denmark and the Netherlands. But leaked American documents revealed that Trudeau told other NATO leaders that Canada had no intention of ever reaching the 2 per cent target.

Defenders of Canada's approach make one good point: whatever Canada might spend on defence, we are always there on the front line when it counts. After Putin's Russia annexed Crimea in 2014, NATO began beefing up its defences. To that end, Canada contributed a small battle group to Latvia, which it has steadily bolstered since then. Initially understrength and ill-equipped, the Canadian-led brigade now has the tanks, artillery, and radar needed to present a credible deterrent.

But the fact remained that, at the end of 2024, Canada remained one of the worst laggards in NATO. In June 2025 Mark Carney announced an immediate increase in defence spending, with further increases planned for future years. We'll see whether he truly commits to modernizing and bolstering Canada's defences or simply joins the long list of prime ministers who talked big but acted small.

Canada is also a laggard within NORAD. That Canada–U.S. agreement dates from 1957 and commits both countries to the joint defence of North American air space. When the terrorists struck New York and Washington on 9/11, the Canadian deputy commander of NORAD was in the command chair. NORAD urgently needs improved radars, sensors, cyber security, and other modern equipment to detect and deter intrusions and threats, and in 2022, Canada committed to spending $39 billion over twenty years toward that modernization. But as of June 2024, the Liberals had spent less than $70 million, a mere fraction of the money that had been budgeted.

Infinite delays in procurement mean that money budgeted for new military acquisitions often goes unspent. Moving from commitment to contracts can take decades. Jean Chrétien's Liberal government favoured the acquisition of the F-35 fighter jet. Stephen Harper's Conservatives committed to the purchase and then backtracked. Trudeau's Liberals cancelled the commitment, held a competition for a replacement fighter, and then once again chose the F-35. The first planes are now scheduled to arrive in 2026, a quarter century after the replacement process began. But now defence experts are warning that the Trump administration, or a future American government, could hobble the aircraft by refusing to send software upgrades and other maintenance. Canada may be better advised to switch to a lower-tech but more dependable European fighter. Will the F-35 imbroglio ever end?

In the same vein, the River-class Destroyer Project, intended to replace aging Halifax-class frigates, has ballooned in cost to an estimated $84 billion, making it one of the most expensive military procurements in Canadian history. The navy's submarine fleet, originally purchased used from the British in the 1990s, has spent more time in dry dock than at sea. These failures underscore a fundamental inability to equip the military in a timely and cost-effective manner.

The lack of soldiers, sailors, and aircrew is also critical. Even if Canada miraculously solved its never-ending procurement disaster, who's going to operate the new equipment? The Armed Forces are bleeding personnel, recruitment is plummeting, and the divide between the military and civilian Canada has never been wider. The country that once floated the third-largest navy in the world now struggles to fill its depleted ranks. The most immediate reason? Money. Serving in uniform has always been tough, but at least there used to be decent pay, benefits, and a pension at the end of it. Now? Some Canadian soldiers are so underpaid they qualify for welfare in some cities. News reports reveal that military personnel are using food banks. The men and women in uniform tasked with defending the country are struggling to afford basic living expenses. Access to health care, mental health support, and family benefits has been gutted. Veterans Affairs routinely fights former soldiers over injury benefits. Some veterans pay out of pocket for treatments the government refuses to cover. Long-term service is a harder sell than ever.

Then there are the scandals. Repeated revelations of sexual misconduct at the highest levels of command have shattered confidence in the institution. For years, sexual abuse has rotted the military from within. Former Supreme Court judge Marie Deschamps called it endemic in 2015. Another former Supreme Court jurist, Louise Arbour, called for civilian oversight in 2022. Little has changed. The CAF promises reform, holds press conferences, and reshuffles leadership, but the scandals keep coming. Sexual misconduct is not unique to the CAF. What is unique is its inability to deal with it. Investigations take years. Military police lack independence. Cases collapse in court. The result? Young Canadians, especially women, see the military as a dead end, or worse, a threat.

There is also the challenge of changing technology. Many in the military still think they are primarily recruiting trigger pullers. Yes, Canada still needs combat troops, but today, war is as likely to be fought on a screen as it is in a trench. The CAF needs to attract a different kind of recruit, and they won't be drawn to rigid hierarchies. They'll expect work–life balance, flexibility, and autonomy, values that clash with a top-down command structure. They'll also expect to live in cities, where jobs and opportunities and nightlife can be found. The military offers deployments to Cold Lake, Wainwright, and Gagetown. Guess how that's working out? The private sector also has a labour shortage. Why risk your life in uniform when you can make more money in tech, health care, or the trades? Past generations saw the military as a stepping stone. This one sees it as a sacrifice—one they're unwilling to make.

The result? A country that can't defend itself. Canada is exposed, hoping its allies, especially the United States, will fight for it when the time comes. But America appears to be moving from ally to antagonist.

❋

Donald Trump arrived in office in his second term with all the experience he'd gained in the first, and with none of the checks and balances the Deep State had imposed on him during that time. He is Trump unbound, and one of his prime targets is Canada. In November, soon after he won the election, Trump vowed to impose 25 per cent tariffs on Canadian and Mexican exports to the United States.

In a phone call to Trudeau on the morning in February when the tariffs were to take effect, Trump cited a litany of complaints, including Canada's unwillingness to pay its share in the upgrading of NORAD defences. And he referred ominously to the 1908 treaty between the United States and Great Britain that established the Canada–U.S. border. The United States, he implied, could withdraw from that treaty. This, of course, is nonsense. As Trudeau reminded Trump, Canada had achieved full sovereignty in the years since then.

But hard facts remain: One is that the president and his advisers appear determined to reshore the North American auto sector, which could devastate manufacturing in southern Ontario. Another is that Canada has critical minerals needed to sustain American manufacturing. Trump has predicted that he could convince Canadians to become part of the United States through "economic force," as he called it in January 2025. Trump is a zero-sum negotiator. He likes to leverage whatever power he has to take things from others. And as president of the United States, he has more power than anyone in the world.

To be clear: Trump would be imposing tariffs even if Canada were spending 2 per cent of GDP on defence and meeting its commitments to NORAD. But the world is changing at a time when Canada is dangerously weakened. Russia is newly aggressive and belligerent. China hungrily eyes Taiwan. The NATO members of Europe are rearming. So are non-European allies such as Australia, which has entered into an agreement with the United States and Great Britain to develop nuclear submarines for that country. Canada was not invited to be part of that agreement because everyone knows we have neither the desire nor the ability to play in the big leagues. For the same reason, Canada is not part of the Quad, a security dialogue involving Australia, India, Japan, and the United States.

Other nations of a similar size to Canada have recognized the need to maintain robust defence capabilities. Australia, a nation with fewer people than Canada, is not only getting new subs; it also has a modernized air force equipped with F-35s. Norway, like Canada a northern, sparsely populated nation, maintains a credible deterrent force, including fifth-generation fighters, frigates, and Arctic-capable forces. South Korea, because of its proximity to North Korea, has built a formidable military-industrial complex, manufacturing its own fighter jets, tanks, and submarines. Canada, by contrast, spends far less, depends on allies for key capabilities, and lacks an equivalent long-term strategic vision.

And all eyes are turning to the North. The Arctic is changing. The ice is melting faster than expected, opening new shipping routes that make it easier to travel between Asia, Europe, and North America while also exposing massive reserves of oil, gas, and minerals. As traditional resources run low, countries are looking north for the next big opportunity. Russia has been the most aggressive player. It has built military bases, expanded its fleet of icebreakers, and asserted its claims in the Arctic. The United States is watching closely. It wants to counterbalance Russian influence and maintain security in North America. China is also making moves, calling itself a "near-Arctic power" and fast-tracking its icebreaker construction program, while the Europeans are making moves as well, drawn by economic and environmental interests.

Canada holds a massive stake in this fight. It claims sovereignty over much of the Arctic, including the Northwest Passage. But not everyone agrees. The United States does not fully recognize Canada's control of the passage, China is looking for ways to gain access, and Indigenous communities have their own governance structures, complicating the issue. The Arctic is increasingly becoming a zone of strategic competition, yet Canada remains woefully unprepared to defend its northern sovereignty. The country's Arctic capabilities remain minimal: six lightly armed Arctic patrol ships, no operational submarines capable of Arctic deployment, and a single deep-water port at Nanisivik that remains incomplete. Canada's failure to take Arctic security seriously could see its territorial claims eroded by foreign encroachment.

And one final, chilling thought. Thomas Jefferson, the principal author of the American Declaration of Independence and the third president of the United States, once wrote that taking Canada would be "a mere matter of marching."

If he thought that then, what does his successor, the president who has declared that the United States will annex Greenland "one way or another," think today?

Foreign policy is defence policy is trade policy. By neglecting its defences and pursuing incoherent strategies in foreign affairs, we find ourselves with few allies or even customers.

Canada stands alone.

SEVEN

THE ELECTION OF '25

On the morning of Monday, December 16, 2024, Housing Minister Sean Fraser called a press conference to announce he would not be running in the next federal election because he wanted to spend more time with his family. Sure. When a politician declares they are stepping down because their children need them at home, it usually means that politically they're toast. With the polls putting the Conservatives thirty points ahead of the Liberals in Nova Scotia, Fraser was almost certainly toast in his riding of Central Nova. The leadership of the provincial Liberals was up for grabs, so it made cynical good sense for Fraser to exit the federal scene.

The timing of the announcement was deliberate. Finance Minister Chrystia Freeland was scheduled to deliver the fall economic statement later that day. A senior minister announcing he would not run in the next election would be just the latest in an endless litany of bad news for Justin Trudeau's Liberal government. At least Fraser's announcement would get little play, with the political class focused on the latest budget numbers. Then came a question the minister wasn't expecting. "I don't know if you are aware," a reporter said to him, "but the deputy prime minister Chrystia Freeland has just announced her resignation from cabinet." Fraser's head jerked up in surprise. "This is news to me," he replied. "It's the first time I'm hearing the news." The election of '25 was underway.

Not officially, of course. Governor General Mary Simon did not issue the writs of election until three months later. But Freeland's decision put the Liberal Party into permanent campaign mode. The party would choose a new leader and prime minister. Then Donald Trump would upend Canadian politics by announcing stiff tariffs on Canadian exports and promoting annexation, which would lead to the greatest upset in Canada's political history.

And that upset would leave Canada outwardly more united, but in reality more broken.

★

Even now, with everything that has transpired, Trudeau and Freeland's mutual public humiliation remains extraordinary. She had been his number two: international trade minister, foreign affairs minister, finance minister, deputy prime minister, the cabinet minister who led the effort to rescue the North American free trade agreement in Donald Trump's first term as president, the minister who would deal with Trump's threats in his second term. She was indispensable. And she was Trudeau's friend.

Except that the *Globe and Mail* had been running stories since the summer about the prime minister's growing lack of confidence in his finance minister's performance. Trudeau was actively courting Mark Carney, the former governor of the banks of Canada and of England, to replace her, the stories said. Everyone suspected that the source of the leaks was the Prime Minister's Office itself.

Trudeau is the only prime minister in Canadian history to have several former cabinet ministers publish books about their years in government while the prime minister they once served was still in office. Former finance minister Bill Morneau wrote that the only time he had a one-on-one with his prime minister was the day he resigned. Former foreign affairs minister Marc Garneau wrote that "Canada's standing in the world has slipped" on Trudeau's watch, because the country is unable or unwilling to match commitments with actions. As a result, "we are losing credibility."[1] After Trudeau removed Jody Wilson-Raybould as attorney general because she refused to go easy on SNC-Lavalin, a Quebec engineering firm facing fraud charges, she wrote that she was angry with herself for thinking Trudeau was an "honest and good person, when, in truth, he would so casually lie to the public and then think he could get away with it."[2]

At a personal level, Trudeau is notoriously distanced from others. His public charm masks a deep introversion that makes him uncomfortable in small gatherings or one-on-one meetings. True to form, Trudeau gave Freeland the news that she was to be replaced as finance minister by Carney via a

Zoom call. There is no worse enemy than a friend betrayed. Freeland exacted revenge in a way that would cause the prime minister the greatest possible political agony. She announced her decision to resign on the morning she was due to deliver the fall economic statement, while publicly releasing a scathing letter to Trudeau. "For the past number of weeks, you and I have found ourselves at odds about the best path forward for Canada," she wrote. Freeland wanted to focus on "keeping our fiscal powder dry" to prepare for the Trump tariff threat. "That means eschewing costly political gimmicks, which we can ill afford and which make Canadians doubt that we recognize the gravity of the moment."[3] Clearly, she was referring to a recent announcement to temporarily suspend the GST on some goods. The letter was devastating.

Trudeau went to ground, cancelling all scheduled media appearances and then disappearing on a skiing vacation. It took three weeks, and open calls for his resignation from the Ontario, Quebec, and Atlantic caucuses, before a grim-faced prime minister stood in front of Rideau Cottage to announce he was stepping down, citing "internal battles," while proroguing Parliament until the end of March.

At a time of national crisis, Trudeau had left the government and his party effectively leaderless, Parliament in suspension, and a spring election all but certain. If Trudeau had been acting in the national interest, that election would have already occurred. Trump's victory on November 5 had thrown Canada into crisis. The soon-to-be-forty-seventh president was skeptical of NATO, fond of tariffs, and seemingly an acolyte of Russian president Vladimir Putin. The federal government required a strong mandate to confront the situation, not the tired, dispirited Liberal ministry it was saddled with. Trudeau should have called a federal election as soon as Trump won, or the opposition parties should have forced one by defeating the minority government on a motion of non-confidence. But Jagmeet Singh had decided to let the government live.

The NDP had been propping up the Liberals for years through a supply-and-confidence agreement, in which Singh's party supported the government on confidence motions in exchange for Liberal commitments to enact, among other things, national dental care and pharmacare programs. Singh had dissolved the quasi-coalition in September, not wishing to be painted with the same political brush as the moribund Liberals. Yet having terminated the agreement, the New Democrats continued to vote with the government on confidence motions. Pierre Poilievre, with typical cruelty, said Singh wanted to keep Parliament going until he qualified for his MP's pension in February 2025. The real reason, according to those in the know, was that the NDP feared being rendered irrelevant in a Parliament dominated by a large Conservative majority government. This reasoning was deeply flawed.

The true enemy of New Democrats is not the Conservatives but the Liberals, who compete with them for the progressive vote. This was something of which Jack Layton had been well aware. The former NDP leader brought down Stephen Harper's minority government in the spring of 2011, knowing a Conservative majority would be the likely electoral outcome. But he capitalized on the deep unpopularity of Liberal leader Michael Ignatieff to vault the NDP into second place and official opposition status. Justin Trudeau was ultimately about as unpopular as Ignatieff had been. In a fall election, the NDP could have capitalized on that unpopularity. Instead, Singh kept the government alive. Had the NDP forced an election in November 2024 or even earlier, the party might have once again won more seats than the Liberals. Instead, the New Democrats were virtually obliterated on April 28, thanks to Donald Trump and Mark Carney.

From the moment of Freeland's resignation, speculation grew that Carney would run for and win the Liberal leadership. The only person who seemed not to understand this was Freeland herself. She hoped to succeed Trudeau, even though many in the party were furious with her for betraying the leader and forcing his resignation, and even though she had been part of the party's leadership for nine years and that leadership was now deeply disliked by most Canadians. Once the race was underway, Freeland and Carney were joined in the contest by Karina Gould, who had been the youngest woman appointed to cabinet in Canada's history when Trudeau made her minister of democratic institutions in 2017 at the age of thirty. In 2025, she clearly was running to raise her profile in anticipation of a future contest.

Gerry Butts, Trudeau's friend and former principal secretary, was organizing for Carney behind the scenes. Katie Telford, Trudeau's longtime chief of staff, and other advisers in the former PMO were also on board. And as soon as Carney entered the campaign, the polls began to move in the Liberals' favour. By the time he became leader on March 7, and then asked for the dissolution of Parliament, the party had moved into first place.

Now, suddenly, everything that had been working for Poilievre—declaring that "Canada is broken," naming his agenda "Canada First" ("America First" was a Trump slogan), pandering to the convoy protesters, vowing to fire the governor of the Bank of Canada and defund the CBC, promising his ministers would be banned from attending the World Economic Forum—started working against him. But his greatest handicap was himself.

✤

Pierre Marcel Poilievre was born to a teenage unwed mother who gave him up for adoption in 1979. Donald and Marlene Poilievre, both schoolteachers, raised him and his brother Patrick. Marlene was an ardent conservative and took her son to rallies. Before long, Pierre was reading the monetarist economist Milton Friedman and volunteering for the Reform Party. He championed and worked for Stockwell Day, leader of the Canadian Alliance, the successor party to Reform, and ran for and won an Ottawa-area seat in the 2004 election under the banner of Stephen Harper's new Conservative Party.

From the first, he was an attack dog, berating the Liberal government and, once the Conservatives won government, belittling the opposition. He got in trouble for accusing Indigenous people of taking government money while not working to lift themselves up on the very day Harper issued his apology in the House of Commons for the abuses of residential schools. But Harper liked Poilievre's combativeness, and eventually moved him into cabinet.

After Harper lost in 2015, Poilievre lay relatively low while Andrew Scheer and Erin O'Toole led the Conservatives to defeat after defeat. He capitalized on O'Toole's unpopularity and the convoy protests in Ottawa—"Freedom, not fear; truckers not Trudeau"—to capture the party leadership in 2022. To his credit, Poilievre recognized earlier than most politicians, and most central bankers, that the stimulus used to combat the economic impact of the COVID-19 pandemic would fuel inflation. He diagnosed as well the frustrations of younger voters, deprived of job security or the realistic hope of owning their own home. He made inroads with voters of South Asian background, and with blue-collar workers. But most of all, he just kept attacking.

Poilievre loved Question Period. When the House was in session, he would spend much of the morning preparing: working on the questions, anticipating the response, shaping the rebuttal. Like John Diefenbaker before him, the populist Conservative leader was happiest when he was on the offensive. Justin Trudeau gave as good as he got, but the prime minister endured Question Period. Poilievre lived for it.

The day before Chrystia Freeland resigned, the Conservatives were more than twenty points ahead of the Liberals according to most polls. Poilievre had skilfully diagnosed and exploited Canadian concerns about inflation, the cost of housing, chronic deficits, drug dependency, rising crime. The Conservative leader was offering practical answers to intractable problems, and more important, he wasn't Justin Trudeau. That seemed sufficient. But the personal intensity, the political ruthlessness, the ugly contempt for anyone—including any conservatives—not entirely on his side proved fatal when contrasted with Mark Carney.

If Poilievre painted himself as a populist outsider ready to take on the system, Carney was the literal embodiment of that system. He was born in Fort Smith, in the Northwest Territories, and raised in Edmonton, the son of a high school principal. His mother raised her four children before completing university and becoming a teacher herself. Carney was such a good student that he competed in both the English and French *Reach for the Top* teams. He studied economics at Harvard and played backup goalie for the college hockey team.

After a stint at Goldman Sachs to pay off student loans, Carney headed to Oxford to take a Ph.D. in economics. There, he met his wife Diana, a fellow hockey player and economist. He also formed a friendship with Graham Bowley, and later with Bowley's wife, Chrystia Freeland. After Oxford, he returned to Goldman Sachs, rising through the ranks to become managing director of investment banking. But he was more interested in policy than in wealth, and became a deputy director of the Bank of Canada in 2003, later joining the finance department. Stephen Harper appointed him governor of the bank in 2008, shortly before the global financial crisis that was sparked by the misbehaviour of the very investment banks in which he'd worked. Canada came through the crisis relatively unscathed, mostly because previous Liberal governments had enforced a conservative banking culture. But Carney, Stephen Harper, and finance minister Jim Flaherty deserved credit for managing the crisis well.

That reputation for competence in the private financial sector, in the finance department, and as a central banker earned Carney an invitation to become the first non-British director of the Bank of England. It also helped that he projected good looks and a certain charisma—he was dubbed "the George Clooney of finance" in the British press. It was a controversial tenure, not least because Carney involved himself in the Brexit debate by warning that leaving the European Union would send Britain into recession. Also, while he was capable and confident, the British press wrote about his "volcanic temper" and the wariness among staff of not getting on his bad side.[4]

After leaving the bank, he took a senior position with Brookfield Asset Management, became a special adviser to the United Nations on climate change, and, in 2024, agreed to head up Trudeau's task force on economic growth. Carney had reportedly flirted with running for the leadership of the Liberal Party before heading to the Bank of England, and Trudeau now actively sought to bring him into the government. Those efforts led to Freeland's resignation, and to the two of them vying for the Liberal leadership after Trudeau decided to step down. Trump's blusterings before he was inaugurated, and his hostility toward Canada once he became president, ensured Carney's victory.

Mark Carney was a rookie politician—before becoming prime minister, he had never been elected dog catcher. He should have stumbled repeatedly throughout the election campaign, and probably would have, had he been subjected to greater exposure. He clearly has a testy disposition. "Look inside yourself, Rosemary," he responded, when the CBC's Rosemary Barton asked him why he would not publicly disclose his financial assets. "You start from a prior of conflict and ill will."[5] In reply to a question about a *Globe and Mail* report that he had met with Beijing-friendly business representatives, he shot back, "You can't believe everything you read in the *Globe and Mail*."[6] But he avoided the outright hostility Poilievre displayed toward the media. More important, in a time of national crisis, he projected the aura of calm competence that Canadians desperately sought.

Before and during the campaign, the Liberals manifested a breathtaking—if typical—level of arrogance. Carney's first act as prime minister was to announce an end to the consumer portion of the highly unpopular carbon tax. The man who had led a crusade within the corporate sector to fight global warming happily embraced accelerating pipeline projects to bring Canadian oil and gas to markets outside the United States. He promoted as well plans to slim down the public service and increase investments in defence. These were all parts of the Conservative platform. The Liberals purloined them and other planks—from cutting the GST on new housing to increasing spending on defence and much more—without a blush. Carney was unfairly accused in one media report of committing plagiarism in his Ph.D. thesis. But the real plagiarism was the Liberal theft of the Conservative platform.

Donald Trump didn't actively campaign to get Mark Carney elected, but his actions boosted the Liberal leader day after day. He imposed tariffs on steel and aluminum imports, and on autos and auto parts. On several occasions, Carney suspended his campaign and returned to Ottawa to discuss countermeasures with cabinet. "The old relationship we had with the United States, based on deepening integration of our economies and tight security and military cooperation, is over," he said in a sombre statement on March 28. "It's clear the U.S. is no longer a reliable partner."[7] Politically, this was gold. The caretaker conventions, which require that political leaders and public servants avoid major governing decisions during an election campaign, went out the window as Carney left the campaign time and time again to return to Ottawa and act prime ministerial. Liberal Members of Parliament who had jumped ship reboarded. Anita Anand reversed her decision to step down as MP for Burlington. Sean Fraser decided he could see more of his children and still run for re-election in Central Nova.

There was little that Poilievre could do in response. He could not out-Carney Carney in his opposition to Trump. Voters wouldn't believe it, and besides, a substantial minority of his core supporters were also Trump supporters. All he could do was pound the issues, reminding voters that in voting for Carney they would be voting for a fourth consecutive Liberal government. It wasn't that the Conservatives were doing badly. Poilievre polled throughout the campaign at around 38 per cent or better, which in any other election would have been enough for the party to win power. Stephen Harper won in 2006 with only 36 per cent. Trudeau received only 32.6 per cent of the vote in 2021, the lowest level of support ever obtained by a federal party that then formed a government.

But the Liberals consistently polled several points ahead, taking votes from the NDP, who were down in single-digit territory. Progressive voters stampeded to Mark Carney, even though he was positioning the party to the right of Trudeau and stealing one Conservative platform plank after another. In *The Big Shift*, we predicted that the progressives would ultimately coalesce around a single progressive political party in response to the emerging Conservative coalition. In 2025, it appeared they had chosen to coalesce around the Liberals.

And Poilievre's angry, aggressive behaviour, and that of his belligerent campaign manager, Jenni Byrne, came back to haunt him. First of all, there was bad blood between Poilievre's people and Nova Scotia premier Tim Houston. Houston had said during the 2024 provincial election campaign that he was not a federal Conservative. "I'm the leader of the Nova Scotia Progressive Conservatives," he declared. "There is a Conservative Party of Canada. It's a completely different party with its own leader."[8] The remark caused Byrne to phone and berate Houston's advisers. If Pierre becomes prime minister, she warned them, he won't lift a finger to help Houston. Houston reached out to Poilievre to explain, but the call was never returned.

But the greatest, and most damaging, tension existed between Poilievre and Jenni Byrne on the one side, and Ontario premier Doug Ford and Kory Teneycke, his campaign manager through three elections, on the other. Byrne had been in a relationship with Poilievre that lasted a decade, and the two remain friends. Like the Conservative leader, she is smart and talented and takes no prisoners. Relations with the Ford camp had not been warm ever since she'd left her job as the premier's principal secretary in 2019. Ford, who once considered himself part of the unofficial opposition to Justin Trudeau known as The Resistance, had mellowed in his political style. During the pandemic, he worked closely with the federal Liberals, going so far as to call Freeland his "good friend." Pointedly, the premier met with Mark Carney once he became prime minister, but made no effort to reach out to Poilievre. But Poilievre had made no effort to reach out to Ford, whom he considered a Conservative in name only. Worse, as polls showed the Liberals leading in the election campaign, Teneycke began openly criticizing the Poilievre campaign, saying the leader acted too "Trumpy" and accusing the Tories of "campaign malpractice" in blowing such an enormous lead so quickly.[9] When Ford was asked about Teneycke's criticism, he replied, "Sometimes the truth hurts."[10]

Some federal Conservatives muttered darkly that Ford aspired to lead the Conservative Party. But shunning Ford damaged Poilievre's prospects. The voters he needed to win over were the voters who have supported the Ontario premier through three elections. Besides, a successful politician cultivates potential allies. There was no need to alienate Ford or Houston, and every good reason to court them. But for Poilievre and Byrne, people are either with them or against them, and those deemed against them were completely frozen out.

On the other hand, there might not have been anything Poilievre could have done to win the election of 2025. He campaigned relentlessly, drew big and enthusiastic crowds, and performed well in both the French- and English-language debates. On election day, the party secured 41.3 per cent of the vote, the highest level of support in the Conservative Party of Canada's history and the highest for any federal conservative party since Brian Mulroney's massive Progressive Conservative victory in 1984. Poilievre's Conservatives took seats from the NDP in Windsor and on Vancouver Island, and even snatched a few seats from the Grits in the 905.

But Mark Carney's Liberals sat at 43.8 per cent, with gains in Quebec and solid support in the 905 and Lower Mainland. The Bloc Québécois lost ten seats, and Singh's NDP were eviscerated, with 6.3 per cent of the vote and seven seats, five short of party status in the House. Singh was defeated in his own riding. But then so was Poilievre, in his riding of Carleton.

The Conservatives had tossed out both Andrew Scheer and Erin O'Toole after their election losses. But in the wake of the 2025 election defeat there was no one within or outside the Conservative caucus prepared to rally support against Pierre Poilievre. He was likely to remain the party's leader. But what future could he or the party look forward to?

❉

Election night revealed several truths. First, Mark Carney, though a rookie politician, was an extremely capable one, pulling off a political miracle—with an assist by Donald Trump— that took the Liberal Party from potential extinction to an almost-majority government victory. Second, the election revealed and worsened deep regional divisions. The Liberals took only two seats in Alberta and only one in Saskatchewan. The election left a lot of people angry. Conservative stalwarts in the Prairie provinces were sick and tired of having their votes negated by suburban voters in Ontario, who supported a political party that showed no understanding of or interest in the Western culture and economy outside the Lower Mainland.

Another truth was that Canada was divided, not just horizontally by region but vertically by generation. An Ipsos exit poll on election night revealed that Canadians fifty-five and older gravitated toward the Liberals, whom they considered best able to contain Donald Trump's threats to Canada's economy and sovereignty—and to the security of their property equity, investment portfolios, and pensions. They called it patriotism and put a flag in the window of their comfortable, mortgage-free homes. But voters under thirty-five considered affordability and the cost of living the chief issues, and they gravitated toward the Conservatives. Many of them had no property equity or pensions to protect. It's harder to love Canada when the country offers you so little and demands so much.

Class cleavages were there as well. The Conservatives took from the NDP several ridings with a large blue-collar work-force. The party also had strong support from private-sector unions. As the NDP vote evaporated, the Conservatives earned the support of those without university degrees and office jobs, while among the educated elites, the Liberals were the majority choice.

Far from bringing Canada together in united opposition to the challenge of the Trump presidency, the election of '25 revealed how far apart Canadians were from each other, and how close Canada had come to reaching its breaking point.

EIGHT

LESSONS FROM '25: CONSERVATIVES

Those attempting to draw lessons from the federal election of 2025 need to remember one thing above all: the election was a freak.

If Kamala Harris had won the presidency in November 2024, everything would have been different. Canada–U.S. relations would have been at the bottom of a long list of priorities focused primarily on the need for lower taxes, income security, and affordable housing. Justin Trudeau might or might not have remained as PM; if he had resigned, Mark Carney might or might not have entered the race to succeed him. But Carney's prospects would have been far less promising, given that he would have been leading a highly unpopular government seeking a fourth term. Trump's win, and his astonishing belligerence toward Canada, sent the apple cart tumbling downhill toward a Liberal victory.

Before that tumble, the Conservatives were on the cusp of government. They had crafted an agenda based on lower taxes, less federal spending, and help for first-time home buyers. They promised to shrink the public service, renew national defence, and toughen bail and parole. There were other, less attractive elements to the platform, which we will examine, but in the main the Conservative message was coherent and attractive to middle-class suburban voters in different regions, of different generations, and of different income levels.

From 2004, when Stephen Harper forged the Conservative Party of Canada, until today, that party has been competitive in every federal election. As we noted, in the 2025 election it received a greater share of the popular vote than Harper's Conservatives achieved in their 2011 majority-government victory. Yet the Conservatives lost. Older, middle-class suburban voters abandoned them for Mark Carney in the face of Donald Trump's threats. Now, the Conservatives need to avoid learning the wrong lessons. Yes, there are problems that need fixing. But the worst mistake could be for Conservatives to attempt a complete remake of a party that, despite recent losses, remains more competitive and makes more sense than at any time since John A. Macdonald was its leader.

In the twentieth century, victories by conservative parties at the federal level had two things in common: first, the victory was a landslide; second, everything ended in grief. In 1930, frustrated voters turned to R.B. Bennett's Conservatives once it became clear that Liberal prime minister Mackenzie King had little grasp of and no solutions for the growing economic crisis that followed the stock market crash of 1929. The Tories won soundly in both the popular vote (Conservatives: 48 per cent; Liberals 44 per cent) and the seat count (Conservatives: 137; Liberals 89). But five years later, Bennett went down to humiliating defeat, winning only thirty-nine seats and 30 per cent of the popular vote. A renascent Mackenzie King would govern for the next thirteen years, followed by nine more years of Liberal rule under Louis St. Laurent.

After those twenty-two years of Liberal hegemony, John Diefenbaker's Progressive Conservatives finally broke through with a minority government in 1957. When the Liberals, under their new leader, Lester Pearson, questioned the legitimacy of the PCs as a government, Diefenbaker gleefully took the question to the people, winning the largest majority government in Canadian history, with 54 per cent of the popular vote and 208 seats. But within five years, the Liberals were back in charge under Pearson, and would stay in charge, apart from Joe Clark's brief interregnum in 1979, for the next two decades.

Brian Mulroney put an end to the Liberal hegemony with another whopping majority-government win in 1984: 211 seats and 50 per cent of the popular vote. He even won a second majority government, fought on the issue of free trade with the United States. But in 1993, the PCs were reduced to two seats, with the Liberals under Jean Chrétien and then Paul Martin set to govern for the next thirteen years.

The lessons were clear: from 1930 to 2006, Conservatives only won elections when voters became sick and tired of seemingly endless Liberal rule. That revulsion produced landslide victories for the Tories, but sooner or later victory was followed by a crushing and long-lasting defeat. The reason for

those defeats was simple: Conservative governments made
no sense. The caucus typically consisted of nationalist MPs
from Quebec, populist conservatives from the West, and Red
Tories from Ontario. Neither Bennett nor Diefenbaker nor
Mulroney could hold together such an unruly and contra-
dictory mob. As internal tensions surfaced, popular support
eroded and voters returned to the Liberal fold. The twentieth
century was a Liberal century, and the twenty-first century
seemed destined to repeat the pattern.

Then Stephen Harper came along and changed the course
of Canada's political history.

Harper, who orchestrated the amalgamation of the Canadian Alliance (formerly Reform) and Progressive Conservative parties into the Conservative Party of Canada, was the
first genuinely conservative Conservative leader, a champion
of smaller government, lower taxes, and fewer regulations.
Diefenbaker and Mulroney operated within the Laurentian
policy consensus of their time. Pearson was able to swiftly
enact medicare because Diefenbaker had already done all
the groundwork; the Liberals initially opposed Mulroney's
free trade agreement with the United States but eventually
embraced it. Harper was different from his predecessors: a
firmly economic conservative who could also accommodate
moderate social conservatives within the tent. There was even
a populist streak in Harper's coalition: the little guy against
the fat cats. Harper conservativism stood for seeking the lowest possible tax rate while balancing the budget, for looking
at ways to slim the bureaucracy and the rules they enforced,
for putting criminals in jail and keeping them there, and for
exploiting oil and gas and other natural resources.

Harper's Conservative base was regional as well as ideo-
logical. A great many people in Alberta and Saskatchewan,
along with rural British Columbia, Manitoba, and Ontario,
embraced the values of the Harper Conservative Party. Those
values were not shared by most in Quebec outside the Beauce
region, or by many in Atlantic Canada. The progressive parties
competed for support in the city centres of Central Canada
and the Lower Mainland. The key to power for the Harper
Conservatives was convincing suburban voters in both regions
to join with their rural and Prairie cousins.

Harper and Immigration Minister Jason ("curry-in-a-hurry")
Kenney courted suburban immigrant voters with policies that
appealed to them—everything from cutting the GST to offering tax credits for children's skates—and by cultivating the
shared conservative values of Asian immigrants and other car-
commuting suburbanites. By 2011, Harper had his majority
government, and that government owned the 905 and suburban Vancouver.

Harper lost in 2015, in part by alienating the very immigrant voters he had courted. But he had bequeathed a legacy no previous federal Conservative leader could claim.
The Conservative Party of Canada made sense. Its base was
solid, its finances robust; it would be competitive in any given
federal election. Indeed, it won the popular vote in the elections of 2019 and 2021 and surpassed 40 per cent of the vote
in 2025.

All successful political parties learn from losing an election. One lesson learned from Election 2025 is that the Conservative coalition is large and coherent, but it needs to grow:
not by much, but enough to capitalize on voter discontent to

win more suburban seats. How does it do that? By adhering to three maxims. Let's look at each one.

❈

First, ignore the crazies. Pierre Poilievre lost the election because many Canadians believed he was a pale imitation of Donald Trump. That wouldn't have mattered so much, had Trump not won a second term. He might even have gotten away with it had Trump not threatened Canada's economy and sovereignty. But once Trump became an antagonist in the Canadian election, every populist trope that Poilievre had indulged in to placate his party's base came back to haunt him.

In Canada, there are economic conservatives who are committed to low taxes, reduced government spending, and balanced budgets. Then there are social conservatives, who embrace the primacy of the family and faith, respect for institutions, and strict adherence to law and order. There are also defence and foreign policy conservatives, who support a strong military, a robust Western alliance, and global free trade. Then there are the crazies.

They come in various shades. Some go beyond wanting to limit immigration to wanting to keep Canada Christian and white. Some go beyond questioning the value of globalization to asserting conspiracies about cosmopolitan elites—they mean Jews—trying to rule the world. Some go beyond support for families to encouraging, or even demanding, higher birth rates, while rejecting the equality of women and of sexual and gender minorities.

Most of the people in the Conservative base are decent, solid folk who contribute to their community and make good neighbours. But a few of them hold unwelcome views. These are the most radical fringe within the party. They are the crazies, the base of the base. To the extent that a Conservative leader nods in their direction, that leader alienates everyone else. Poilievre never openly courted the crazies, but he winked at them knowingly from time to time. He promised to defund the CBC. He questioned the legitimacy of some transgender concerns. He vowed that none of his ministers would attend the World Economic Forum. He called diversity, equity, and inclusion policies "garbage."[1] He said he would fire the governor of the Bank of Canada. The broader public may support a few of these policies, but for most Canadians, economic concerns matter far more. For the base of the base, though, this is all red meat.

Conservative strategists reason that such nudge-nudge, wink-wink, say-no-more, say-no-more catering to the base of the base is necessary to keep them within the Conservative tent. The calculation is that unless they have a voice within the party, they will drift over to Maxime Bernier's People's Party. Bernier sings to the base of the base. He wants sharply lower levels of immigration and opposes multiculturalism. He would ban late-term abortions and opposes "gender ideology." Growing opposition to vaccine mandates, and to Conservative Leader Erin O'Toole's support for a carbon price, helped Bernier's party secure almost 5 per cent of the vote in the 2021 election—some of it, no doubt, belonging to conservatives who realized O'Toole could not win and so decided to vote "none of the above." But with Pierre Poilievre at the helm, they drifted back. The PPC secured less than 1 per cent of the vote on April 28.

But winning back the base of the base cost the Conservatives in suburban Ontario. Kory Teneycke was wrong to say that Poilievre had to focus more on attacking Donald Trump. There was no way for the Conservative leader to win that contest against someone like Mark Carney. But Doug Ford's campaign manager was right when he dubbed the Poilievre campaign "Trumpy." Poilievre told crowds of enthusiastic supporters that "Canada is broken." Trump said Canada made no sense except as an American state. Poilievre's contempt for the media echoed Trump's contempt. Most of all, he supported the convoy protests, which for many seemed like a watered-down imitation of the January 6 attack on Congress.

Poilievre's Canada-is-not-for-sale language was every bit as tough as Carney's, as was his eminently sensible core message: that Canada had been in trouble long before Trump was elected, and the best way to fend off the impact of tariffs was through vigorous conservative reform of the federal government and the national economy. But there was no denying he gave off a Trumpesque vibe. He came to the Conservative Party from the right wing, having worked for the Reform Party and for Stockwell Day. Jenni Byrne was once a friend of Erin O'Toole's. But she turned on him, working to ensure that leader's defeat after the 2021 election, because she believed he had become what Margaret Thatcher called "a wet": someone who calls themselves a conservative but shies away from truly conservative principles. In the U.S., they are called RINOs—Republicans in name only.

Poilievre is by no means a member of the base of the base. His wife Anaida is an immigrant from Venezuela. (She was a great asset on the campaign trail.) He learned the challenges of raising a special-needs child. (Valentina is nonverbal.) His adoptive father came out as gay and sat with his partner in the hall as his son became Conservative leader. Poilievre listened with genuine empathy as supporters told him about their struggles to pay rent and still find money for groceries. But the Pierre Poilievre the voters saw was a hard-edged right-wing warrior. Fine, if the alternative was Justin Trudeau. Not so fine when it was Mark Carney and when the issue for millions of voters became saving Canada from Donald Trump.

By nodding to the crazies, Poilievre alienated the suburban Central Canadian and B.C. voters he needed for victory. Also, he violated the second maxim for Conservative victory: get beyond angry. There is good reason for anger: at Central Canadian indifference to the needs and aspirations of the Prairie West; at Liberal indifference to economic growth and improved productivity; at ridiculous housing prices and a gig economy that keeps people living on the edge of their paycheque; at a bloated federal public service, at a failing health care system, at taxes that deliver not enough bang for the buck.

But anger is not enough. Conservatives must have a clear sense of how they can deliver a better life for Canadians. Poilievre's supporters would argue that he had exactly that plan, one so skilfully crafted that the Liberals made off with it and called it their own. But the platform mattered less than the personality and presence of the leader. For two years, he had been railing against the incompetence and corruption of

Justin Trudeau. But Trudeau was gone, and a grave former central banker promised to protect Canadian interests. Poilievre's angry rhetoric now started to backfire. Anger, beyond a certain point, is toxic, because it undermines the possibility of hope.

Which brings us to the third maxim for a federal Conservative win: be pragmatic. Poilievre and his aides had no time for the wishy-washy conservatism of Doug Ford and Tim Houston. But Ford and Houston have won successive elections. Over the decades, conservative governments in the Western provinces have adopted a centre-right approach that emphasizes the centre as much as the right. Again, Poilievre's language was stronger than his policies: his platform envisioned no immediate return to balanced budgets, for example. But by employing strongly populist conservative tropes, he made some voters fearful.

Beyond these maxims—ignore the crazies, get beyond angry, be pragmatic—lies the most important question of all facing Pierre Poilievre: Can he grow? The Conservative leader boasts that the values he laid out in an essay he wrote in high school are the same values he has held through life and that he holds now. "The most important guardian of our living standards is freedom," he wrote in 1999: "the freedom to earn a living and share the fruits of our labour with loved ones, the freedom to build personal prosperity through risk-taking and a strong work ethic, the freedom of thought and speech, the freedom to make personal choices, the collective freedom of citizens to govern their own affairs democratically." You can hear his voice in that student essay. You can imagine him saying the same thing today. All well and good, but a successful leader holds to core beliefs while also learning and growing. Has Pierre Poilievre changed in the quarter century since he

wrote that essay? Will he change having lost the 2025 election? Can he grow from that experience? Can he convince us
he has grown?

Stephen Harper embraced fundamental conservative principles as a young man and never abandoned them. But after he
narrowly lost the 2004 election to Paul Martin's Liberals, he
travelled the country, talked to fellow conservatives, reflected
on the lessons he needed to learn, changed his staff, amended
his policies, and brought the Conservatives to victory in 2006,
growing his support in 2008 and 2011. Is Pierre Poilievre capable of that? We may soon find out, because the Conservative
coalition faces a new and dangerous threat to the party and
the country. How Poilievre handles that threat could tell us
whether he is ready to be prime minister.

✤

At one level, Alberta's rising anger stems from little more than
petulance. Had the Conservatives won a majority government in 2025, as they had long been expected to do, there
would have been no talk of a referendum on separation. But
at a deeper level, that anger stretches back almost to the first
days of settlement. In the early years of the twentieth century,
proponents for provincehood argued for a single large province west of Manitoba that would be named Buffalo. Instead,
Wilfrid Laurier created two smaller provinces: Alberta and
Saskatchewan. And those provinces initially lacked control
over their natural resources, which the Eastern provinces
enjoyed. For decades, Westerners resented Central Canadian
indifference toward and domination of the Prairie economy,

as epitomized by Pierre Trudeau's National Energy Program. The policies of Trudeau the younger, emphasizing environmental stewardship over resource development, are no less despised, and it is these resentments that brought UCP premier Danielle Smith to power. The United Conservative Party is not sovereigntist, but there are sovereigntists within the UCP and Smith respects their voices. When Central Canadian and other commentators accuse Smith and her supporters of failing to stand up for a united Canada against Donald Trump, they simply prove the sovereigntists' point.

In truth, there is little threat of Alberta separating from Canada to become a sovereign nation. The movement has failed to throw up a strong leader like René Lévesque, Jacques Parizeau, or Lucien Bouchard, who were leaders of the Quebec sovereignty movement. But there is another possibility: Alberta becoming an American state. And that movement has a powerful leader in Donald Trump.

We know that younger Canadians, lacking economic security, are less committed to the country than older Canadians. We know that many in Alberta and Saskatchewan deeply resent Liberal Central Canadian interference in their affairs. And now a U.S. president has put annexation on the table. Trump is probably just trolling Canadians with his talk of us becoming a fifty-first state. But once annexation is on the agenda, it's impossible to remove it. People in Alberta and Saskatchewan, especially, might be tempted to tell the American president to make an offer, and then demand that offer be put to a referendum.

The federal Liberals, who brought us to this pass, have no difficulty uniting against talk of separation and annexation.

Elbows up! But many Prairie Conservatives are resolved that they will no longer allow their future to be determined by voters in Quebec and suburban Ontario. Sovereigntist or annexationist impulses threaten to fracture the Conservative coalition. It is Pierre Poilievre's challenge to keep it united. In May 2025, Poilievre reiterated that he opposes sovereignty for Alberta but understands the frustrations of its supporters. "Frankly, Albertans have a right to be frustrated," he told reporters. "I think the message to the government in Ottawa, the Liberal government, is you can't tell Alberta to just pay up and shut up."[2] That message will work in the West. Will it work in Ontario?

Keeping the Conservative coalition together means keeping Canada together. Is Pierre Poilievre up to the challenge? Is the Conservative Party? And what about the rest of us?

NINE

LESSONS FROM '25: PROGRESSIVES

At the start of this century, the Canadian right was broken. Progressive Conservatives clung to nostalgia while the Reform Party howled from the sidelines. Between them, they split the vote, lost the country, and let the Chrétien Liberals run the table. But then the squabbling parties swallowed their pride and got serious about winning. Peter MacKay's Progressive Conservatives united with Stephen Harper's Canadian Alliance within a conservative movement that largely abandoned the Red Tory legacy.

The Conservative Party of Canada dispensed with the old Laurentian electoral formula of dominating urban and suburban Ontario and Quebec. Instead, they based their power on the rising West while also chasing the growing political

influence of immigrant voters. In 2011, Harper won a comfortable majority government despite winning only five seats
in Quebec. He did not need the old consensus; he replaced it.
For a time, he rewrote the rules of Canadian elections.

In those years, it was the progressive vote that fractured,
ensuring Conservative victories. Paul Martin forced out
Jean Chrétien as Liberal leader; Stéphane Dion replaced the
defeated Paul Martin; Michael Ignatieff succeeded the deeply
unpopular Stéphane Dion. Ignatieff reduced the Liberals to
third-place status in the House, with only thirty-four seats
and less than 19 per cent of the popular vote in the 2011
election, even as Jack Layton vaulted the New Democrats to
103 seats and the status of official opposition. In *The Big Shift*,
we predicted that the disunited left would one day merge,
just as the disunited right had merged. Would the rising NDP
swallow the Liberals, or would a rejuvenated Liberal Party
absorb the NDP? Would they combine into a new Liberal
Democratic Party, or would something else arise? One way or
another, we believed, a united progressive party would eventually confront a united Conservative Party, with each credibly
contending for power.

In the years that followed, the progressive parties fell into a
relationship neither was willing to admit. There was no formal
merger, no Harper-and-MacKay-style wedding. But like many
modern couples, the Liberals and New Democrats moved in
together anyway. What started out as a fling of shared political
advantage became something of a domestic arrangement. The
two of them split the bills, raised the policies, and bickered
over who deserved the credit. It was hardly romance, but it
got the job done. The progressive parties are finally learning

what the right embraced a generation ago: in today's political landscape, working together is the only route to power.

❧

Progressive parties—Liberals, New Democrats, Bloc Québécois, and Greens at the federal level—regularly command around 60 per cent of the popular vote. The twenty-first century Conservatives, even firing on all cylinders, rarely crack 40. That gap is not a fluke. It is baked into the electorate. It should have delivered an entrenched progressive hegemony in this century. But it has not, because Canada still uses the first-past-the-post system, in which the candidate with the most votes wins in each contested riding. That Westminster-style system of choosing a legislature often produces majority governments, even though the winning party may not even have won the popular vote overall. Such a system punishes smaller parties. The French political scientist Maurice Duverger mapped out the reasoning in the 1950s. Duverger's law holds that first-past-the-post systems tend to produce two dominant parties. Here's why:

You may believe that the health of the planet should be the highest priority of government, and so you are inclined toward the Green Party. Your spouse may wish for greater social equity, and so is inclined toward the New Democrats. But Duverger's law predicts that on election day both of you will vote Liberal, despite the party's wishy-washy commitments to the environment and social reform, because you fear the Conservatives above all else, and you are afraid of wasting your vote on parties that have no realistic chance of winning

government. Were you in a system with some form of proportional representation, you and your spouse would probably
each vote for your preferred party, hoping that it would form
part of a governing coalition, with its priorities part of the
agenda. In first-past-the-post, many voters cast their ballots
primarily out of fear: fear of Republicans or Democrats in
the United States; of Labour or Conservatives in Britain; of
Labour or Liberals in Australia.

This was as true as ever in the 2015 Canadian election,
when the question of where the progressive vote should go
to stop the Conservatives hung in the balance. The Liberals
were at risk of being permanently eclipsed by a dominant
New Democratic Party, something few would ever have predicted given that party's rocky history.

The roots of social democracy in Canada emerged from the
social gospel movement, a strain of early-twentieth-century
Protestant reform that viewed inequality, poverty, and injus-
tice as moral failures to be corrected through collective action.
The Co-operative Commonwealth Federation and its successor, the New Democratic Party, were dedicated to that social
purpose. But social purpose carries with it a weakness: it values
being right more than being in power.

Tommy Douglas, the father of medicare in Canada, made
little progress as the first leader of the NDP in the 1960s.
Many people admired Ed Broadbent and wanted to vote for
him in the 1980s, but the country-defining debate over free
trade with the United States once again pushed the New
Democrats to the sidelines. Things were grim in the 1990s,
with the NDP at one point losing party status in the House of
Commons. Then along came Jack Layton.

Layton first established his reputation as a high-profile Toronto city councillor and long-shot mayoral candidate. He was media-fluent, telegenic, bilingual, and comfortable in the national spotlight long before he ever entered federal politics. Elected leader in 2003, he brought charisma, urban polish, and political hunger to the party. He repositioned the NDP as a credible progressive alternative to the Liberals, especially in cities and among younger voters. Layton's style was less doctrinaire and more pragmatic than some of his predecessors. He leaned into the party's moral tradition while also creating an election machine built to grow, not just survive. In 2006 and 2008, the party made gains. And 2011 changed everything.

As we've noted, Layton voted with the other opposition parties that year to bring down the Harper government, knowing that a Conservative majority would be the likely outcome, because he believed that the Liberals, not the Conservatives, were the real enemy of the NDP. He aimed to displace the Liberals from the left, just as Stephen Harper aimed to displace them from the right. Layton had already recruited Thomas Mulcair, a former cabinet minister in the Quebec Liberal government, to run in a by-election and join the NDP caucus. Layton and Mulcair converted both Ignatieff's and Harper's unpopularity in Quebec into a stunning surge, an Orange Wave that delivered a national total of 103 NDP seats and opposition-party status. Suddenly the NDP was not a conscience but a contender.

The NDP leader was, however, fatally ill with prostate cancer and died that August. Mulcair, his successor, sought to build on Layton's momentum by making the NDP look like a government in waiting, an approach that appeared to be working. The party vied for first place in the polls when Harper called the election for October 19, 2015. With a leader who looked prime ministerial and a platform based on a balanced budget, the NDP had strong support in Quebec and a realistic shot at winning seats in Ontario. But Mulcair underestimated Justin Trudeau, just as Stephen Harper and so many others underestimated Pierre Trudeau's eldest son.

Trudeau inherited a party with shaky finances, a shaky organization, and a shaky political future. His solution to rescuing the party was to move it to the left of the NDP, promising deficit-fuelled social spending, Indigenous reconciliation, a commitment to fight global warming, and an end to the first-past-the-post system—though that last promise he betrayed. The electorate was done with the Conservatives, and as it turned out, Mulcair was no match for Trudeau in an election campaign. The NDP leader seemed dull and grey beside the coiffed and charming upstart. The Liberals won a comfortable majority government, reducing the Conservatives to opposition status and putting the NDP back in third place. Once in government, Trudeau set about replacing the NDP as the truly progressive party. The NDP, unwittingly, did all it could to help.

❧

Delegates, angry at Mulcair for failing to deliver government and for instead returning the NDP to third-party status, voted to remove him as leader. This was a stunning move for a party known for loyalty and patience. There was no scandal.

No collapse. Just disappointment. This set the stage for Jagmeet Singh. Charming, stylish, and the first person of colour to lead a major federal party, Singh won the leadership in 2017 promising generational change and progressive renewal. But he proved to be inexperienced and unpopular with his caucus. Most important, he never answered the central question: Was the NDP hoping to govern, as it had after Jack Layton's breakthrough, or was it content merely to influence?

The NDP under Singh reverted to its familiar role: a distant-third, also-ran party that nonetheless influenced a minority Liberal government. At least, that's how it seemed. In reality, the NDP was pushing the Liberals to where Justin Trudeau already wanted to go. After the 2021 election, the two parties negotiated the supply-and-confidence agreement in which the NDP supported the Liberals in exchange for NDP demands for new national pharmacare and dental care programs from the governing party. Trudeau was happy to oblige, and to also add a national childcare program, the greatest expansion of the social safety net since his father had been prime minister.

The old cliché is that Liberals campaign from the left and then govern from the centre. Justin Trudeau shattered that cliché. He campaigned from the left and then governed from the further left. In the 2015 campaign, he promised modest deficits. "Modest" turned out to be $18 billion in 2017, $325 billion in the pandemic year of 2020, and $62 billion at the end of fiscal 2024. His government not only implemented the Supreme Court's mandate to permit medical assistance in dying, it turned Canada into a world leader, if that's the right word, in assisted suicide. He legalized marijuana, legislated

protection for the transgendered, sent immigration levels
through the roof, and apologized and apologized and apologized.

He remade the Liberal Party into the epicentre of Canadian progressivism. Climate action, Indigenous reconciliation,
gender politics, abortion rights, identity politics, and muscular
government intervention all became Liberal territory. During
the pandemic, he made vaccine mandates the litmus test of
social responsibility. He wrapped his politics in moral urgency,
casting Conservatives not just as wrong but as a threat to
everything that any good Canadian ought to believe in. Voting
Liberal was no longer a compromise; it was a moral obligation
for many progressive Canadians.

Trudeau was ruthless in appropriating NDP and Green
policies and priorities. If you feared global warming, how
could you possibly not vote Liberal in support of its carbon
tax? If you supported publicly financed childcare or pharmacare or dental care, how could you possibly not vote for the
party that had delivered all three programs? Progressive
critics accused the Conservatives of polarizing politics, but
Trudeau was a polarizer-in-chief. As he saw it, to oppose
Liberal policies was to oppose science, or public health, or
global warming.

He accompanied this agenda with a ruthless form of executive federalism. Liberals had always chafed at provincial
responsibility under the constitution for social services and
natural resources. Trudeau wielded the federal fiscal stick with
determination. If the provincial governments wanted increased
funding for health care, they had to oblige by increasing support for mental health and other Liberal priorities. If the

provincial governments weren't willing to cooperate in fighting global warming, their citizens would be faced with a federal carbon tax. And speaking of global warming, it was time for federally imposed limits on resource extraction, especially from the oil sands. This enraged the Alberta and Saskatchewan governments, but who cared what they thought?

All of this left the NDP with a grave dilemma. The party that once defined itself as the social conscience of Parliament found itself marginalized by a Liberal Party that had invaded its turf. The Liberals under Justin Trudeau spoke the NDP's language and championed the NDP's policies. Singh insisted that his supply-and-confidence agreement had forced the Liberals to enact NDP priorities. But voters well knew the truth: those policies were Liberal priorities, or at least the priorities of Justin Trudeau.

In many ways, this was conventional Liberal rule, just with flashier socks. Justin Trudeau governed with the same structural instincts as his father and the same Duverger playbook. Strong executive federalism. Big deficits. Industrial policy. Ambitious national programs that pushed deep into provincial space and that hijacked NDP policies. A federal government that set the priorities, wrote the cheques, and defined the national agenda.

But there was one major difference. Pierre Trudeau's brand of identity politics was aimed squarely at Quebec. He fought to reconcile the province's distinctiveness within a unified Canadian framework. Justin Trudeau's version of identity politics was global in origin, focused on structural oppression, intersectionality, and moral obligations toward historically marginalized groups. Indigenous reconciliation was a major part of this approach, but the real centre of gravity was the cosmopolitan progressivism of international NGOs, elite universities, and social justice movements. It played well in urban Canada. It did not play well in Quebec.

That is the irony. The province Pierre Trudeau spent his career trying to anchor within Canada is fundamentally opposed to his son's moral world view. Quebec's laws on state secularism stand in direct conflict with the multicultural, rights-based identity politics Justin Trudeau championed. For many Quebecers, identity means language, history, and secular public space. It does not mean diversity, equity, and inclusion. It is difficult to imagine a sharper contrast. Federalism versus nationalism, social spending versus fiscal prudence, climate ambition versus economic caution—none of it moves the needle if it does not speak to Quebec's identity and autonomy. The Bloc Québécois positions itself as the permanent defender of Quebec's distinct status. It does not need to win power. It only needs to protect the nation within the nation.

The Liberals dominate the other side of the map in Quebec. They consolidate the urban, multicultural, progressive vote. They speak the language of climate action, social justice, and institutional inclusion. These are core values for many voters in and around Montreal. The Liberal brand is not without friction in Quebec, but it is familiar and stable. These are tribal realignments. The Bloc holds the nationalist vote. The Liberals hold the progressive vote. And the others are mostly fighting for scraps.

Quebec may be its own political ecosystem, but the rest of the country is catching up. What has long been true in that province—voters choosing the best vehicle to stop the outcome they fear—defines federal politics more broadly. The 2025 federal election proved the logic of strategic consolidation more clearly than ever.

※

According to an Ipsos election day survey of nine thousand voters conducted for Global News, 42 per cent of Liberal supporters said they voted for the party not because they liked the platform or the leader, but because they wanted to stop someone else. Most of the time, that someone was a Conservative. This is what Duverger's law looks like. Voters who preferred the NDP or the Greens backed the Liberals instead, not because they wanted to, but because they felt that they had to. For them, the threat of Trump trumped all else. Elbows up, they ticked the Liberal box. Among those who voted NDP in 2021 but switched in 2025, four times as many moved to the Liberals as to the Conservatives. That is not drift. That is migration. The Liberals did not just hold their base, they raided someone else's.

But the NDP lost ground to the right as well. Conservatives took NDP seats in industrial and resource-heavy ridings that once flew the orange banner. These were not traditional Tory strongholds; these were towns built on union wages and hard hats. But the voters who live there, especially younger men without university degrees, are no longer buying what the NDP is selling. They are not marching downtown with the social justice crowd. They are heading to the ballot box with different concerns and different loyalties.

This is the squeeze play. The Liberals attract strategic progressives. The Conservatives attract working-class realists. And the NDP is left talking to itself. It wears a moral halo, but voters have stopped looking up. Things might have gone in the opposite direction had Singh pulled the plug in the fall of 2024. But in choosing to keep the Liberal government alive, he doomed his future and perhaps the future of the party itself. That may be his real legacy.

It is no longer unthinkable that what is left of the NDP caucus could one day cross the floor to the Liberals. Nor is it implausible that the NDP and Liberals could one day formalize a merger: a new progressive machine for federal politics. So is this, finally, the unification of the progressive movement within a single party, responding to the decades-old consolidation of the conservative movement within the Conservative Party? Perhaps, but perhaps not.

The Liberals are a national party only on paper. They are virtually shut out of Alberta and Saskatchewan. Their support in rural Canada is negligible. They pushed back the Bloc, at least temporarily, in Quebec in the last election and continue to dominate in Atlantic Canada, but there are large swaths of this country where, to reverse an old joke of John Diefenbaker's, the only thing protecting the Liberals is the game laws.

Meanwhile, the NDP remains viable provincially. In British Columbia, David Eby won government in 2024, narrowly surviving a challenge from a revived Conservative Party. In Manitoba, the NDP returned to government in 2023 under Wab Kinew. As of June 2025, the party was the official opposition in Alberta, Saskatchewan, Ontario, and Nova Scotia.

Across much of the country, the NDP is the dominant progressive brand on the ground. It has infrastructure, activists, and a real electoral base.

But federally, the NDP cannot convert provincial strength into national relevance. The reasons are not personal. They are structural. The voters who support the NDP provincially shift to the Liberals federally or stay home. It had its moment under Jack Layton and Tom Mulcair, but the party no longer looks like a government in waiting. And voters do not hand power to a party unsure of itself.

The Liberals, for their part, win federal elections but lack meaningful provincial depth outside Atlantic Canada. In the summer of 2025, they governed only in Newfoundland and Labrador and New Brunswick. Elsewhere, the party is increasingly invisible. They are the third party in the Ontario legislature. In Alberta and Saskatchewan, they hold not a single provincial seat. In Manitoba, they hold one. In British Columbia, they have effectively been absorbed by the Conservatives. In Quebec they are shadows of their former selves.

Provincial politics outside Quebec increasingly appears to be evolving into the sort of two-party system seen in other first-past-the-post systems: the NDP versus some brand of Conservatives. But there is no federal progressive party—yet. Progressive parties at the federal level compete for the same voters, in the same places, with no coordination and no shared purpose.

By contrast, the Conservative movement operates like a political confederation. The provincial and federal parties have different names—the Saskatchewan Party, the United Conservative Party, the Progressive Conservative Party—but they draw from the same pool of candidates, donors, and campaign professionals. When they fight, it is usually a family feud, such as the feud between the Progressive Conservatives and the Conservatives to see who is more powerful in Ontario.

In 2025, Pierre Poilievre could not stem the flight of urban boomers and Gen Xers to Mark Carney. But the Conservative Party of Canada is built to survive a loss and fight again. The conservative movement in Canada is strong federally and dominant provincially. The left, in contrast, is still circling the question of how to unite. Eventually, it must choose. Progressives must learn to work together against the conservatives at every level in every election.

If they fail to choose, their movement could fail as well.

TEN

A CRISIS OF CRISES

Every country faces difficult times. But some times are more difficult than others. There are times when challenges don't arrive in isolation but in waves—colliding, overlapping, each reinforcing the other. For Canada, this is such a time: a moment not of concern, or even crisis, but of national reckoning.

This has always been a hard country to hold together: more improvised than inspired, more negotiated than created. We were never united. Instead, on the edge of one empire, we confederated to avoid being swallowed by another. All things considered, the country has worked well: filling a cold northern half of a continent with immigrants; making farms, then factories, then offices. We have fought wars and overcome hard times and given the world everything from insulin to peacekeeping to peanut butter to the BlackBerry.

But things are not working well now. Incrementally, but unmistakably, the institutions that once held us together are straining under the weight. A health care system once viewed with pride now forces patients to wait for hour after hour in emergency rooms and has left more than six million people across the country without access to a family doctor. National test scores in math, science, and reading have been declining for more than two decades. Canada has the worst productivity growth in the OECD. And the consensus on immigration has fallen apart. There are no riots in the streets. Our politics remain relatively civil, although our legislatures have become more theatre than substance. But tensions are rising in every region, with the West especially estranged.

And for an entire generation, the Canadian dream has become a cruel joke. In many places, the average home now costs more than anyone with an average income can afford. The percentage of people aged twenty-five to twenty-nine still living with their parents has gone from one in five twenty years ago to almost one in three today. In the 1980s, it was more like one in ten. No wonder Canada's fertility rate has fallen to among the lowest in the developed world. Nearly half of Canadians under thirty-five say they'd leave the country if they could. Young people are not asking how to get ahead, but how to get out.

Our elites, especially the Laurentian elites in Central Canada, treat the resource economy as something of an embarrassment, still chasing the fantasy of a green-tech utopia. And our national identity has faded into something vague and performative, flickering like a radio signal just out of range. Postnational, some call it.

The good news is, we've faced challenges equally grave, and met them. We overcame past threats of annexation and invasion from the United States. We came to the brink of breaking up during two referenda on Quebec succession and survived. What we had then, and desperately need now, is a sense of purpose. We have let too many things drift for too long, so that today we face a crisis of crises. We might have kept on drifting for a few years more, falling a little bit further behind, falling slowly apart. But then a virus arrived and exposed all the cracks.

❦

The COVID-19 pandemic did not just break our health care system, it broke our confidence. Institutions long considered steady and dependable revealed themselves to be fallible, reactive, and even political. We are still carrying the weight of the lockdowns: psychologically, financially, spiritually. Many lost loved ones. Many more lost trust in their governments. To understand what we have been through, we have to look at events with honest eyes.

At the beginning, we were flying blind. No vaccine. No roadmap. No one was even sure how the disease was transmitted. Scientists, politicians, and citizens improvised. The safest approach appeared to be the strictest: lockdowns, school closures, travel bans, distancing. "Follow the science" became a national slogan. But the science was uncertain. Too often, officials presented educated guesses as settled fact. Too often, public safety trumped personal freedom, with little room for honest debate.

COVID spread widely, but it killed selectively. Older adults and people with chronic conditions were most at risk. Yet the public health response treated everyone as equally vulnerable. There was no risk stratification, no nuance. We did real harm to ourselves in trying to protect ourselves. Children lost critical years of development. People's mental health suffered. Yes, this is hindsight. No one knew the risks. But did the bylaw officer really need to fine the mother who took her daughter to the park so the child could play on a swing?

The inequity was especially cruel at long-term care facilities. The institutions meant to protect them were underfunded and overwhelmed. We discovered that the entire long-term care system depended on underpaid and overworked support staff, many of them brought in from overseas. When the pandemic struck, some fled. Others who bravely carried on lacked training or support. In some extreme cases, the military had to be called in. They reported scenes of shocking neglect and mismanagement in some nursing homes.

The toll was not just measured in death. It was measured in loss of dignity. Darrell Bricker's younger brother, Russ, died from cancer during the pandemic. Strict rules meant few family members could be by his side. After he passed, his body was sealed and wheeled out under protocol. His partner played a piper's lament from her phone as a lone funeral-home worker loaded him into a hearse. No funeral. No gathering. No goodbye. Too many Canadians shared some version of that story. The policies may have been necessary, but they deepened the pain.

New class divisions emerged. There was the professional in a three-bedroom home, working remotely and ordering groceries to be delivered. Suddenly, having a backyard and a room that could be converted into an office became invaluable assets. Then there were the frontline health care workers, often exhausted from overwork, risking their lives to treat the ill and the dying. And there were the millions who worked the cash registers, delivered the food, kept the whole system running while risking exposure.

When vaccines arrived, miraculously and quickly, that should have been a turning point. But instead of bringing unity, vaccines became another wedge. On the one side, conspiracy theorists alleged without evidence that the vaccines were unsafe, that they could cause more harm than they prevented. They made these accusations out of fear and to exploit the vulnerable. On the other side, politicians made vaccination not just a safety measure but a moral crusade. Those who refused the vaccine were painted as not just misguided but malevolent. Overall, the policies more or less worked. Canada had one of the lowest mortality rates from COVID of any developed country. But the social cost was enormous, with society polarized over the need for prevention versus the rights of free individuals.

The polarization culminated, in early 2022, in the Freedom Convoy. A protest that began as a response to a new vaccine mandate for truckers grew into a howl of frustration: about lockdowns, about elites, about Justin Trudeau, about not being heard. The protesters turned downtown Ottawa into a living hell, with their horns and exhaust fumes and obscenities. But many Canadians, while opposing the protesters' methods, felt some sympathy for their cause. An Ipsos poll at the time

found that 46 per cent of Canadians saw the frustrations of
the protesters as legitimate. Among eighteen- to thirty-four-
year-olds, it was 61 per cent.

Trudeau, in response, did not engage; he escalated. When
Ottawa police proved unable to control the protests, the
government invoked the Emergencies Act. Protesters were
arrested, bank accounts frozen, tow-truck drivers conscripted.
Was it necessary? Many people in Ottawa thought so. They
wanted their city back. Others, more removed, were not so
sure. A public inquiry found the legal threshold for the government's actions had been met, but the Federal Court later
ruled that the government had violated the Charter.

The Trudeau government and the protesters each fanned
flames—of protest, of power against protest. The country is
still sifting through the ashes. Meanwhile, as the pandemic
ebbed, a new financial plague emerged: the worst inflation and
highest interest rates most people have ever lived through.

❋

Inflation didn't crash through the front door; it slipped in
through the checkout lane, the rent bill, the mortgage renewal.
Price hikes might have been inevitable: government efforts to
protect workers and businesses through massive federal transfers were probably bound to lower the value of all the dollars
they were pumping out. The real transgression was central
bankers refusing to admit that the stimulus, compounded
by disrupted supply lines, was inflationary. When inflation
peaked at more than 8 per cent in July 2022, they seemed

utterly surprised. Central banks responded by raising interest rates to tamp down spending. Those interest rates bit further into incomes as mortgage rates skyrocketed.

By 2025, inflation had cooled to around 2 per cent and interest rates were coming down. But the damage had been done. Prices for basics haven't fallen; they've just stopped rising as quickly. For the average family of four, grocery costs are projected to rise by $801 in 2025. Meat prices are expected to be up another 4 to 6 per cent. The cart still looks half empty. Worse, wages haven't kept pace. Adjusted for inflation, many Canadians are earning less in real terms than they were two decades ago. Today, 85 per cent of people say they're living paycheque to paycheque, according to a study by H&R Block, up from 60 per cent in 2024. Nearly half report they can't save for retirement or afford to buy a home. One in ten can't cover their basic living expenses. Those are not just numbers. They are Canadians living in fear and pain.

Debt, once a temporary fix, has become a way of life. In 2024, 69 per cent of Canadian adults used credit cards to pay for essentials such as groceries, gas, and utilities, according to the Canadian Consumer and Credit Report. A third of them couldn't pay off the full balance each month. By early 2025, Canadian consumer debt hit a record $2.5 trillion. Credit card balances were up more than 9 per cent year over year. And mortgages now account for three quarters of all household debt.

Canada's household debt-to-GDP ratio is the highest in the G7. We borrow more, relative to the size of our economy, than Americans, Brits, Germans, Italians, or the Japanese. And with interest rates still sharply higher than in 2022, the cost of carrying that debt has grown heavier. Homeowners are seeing their mortgage payments spike on renewal. Renters aren't faring much better. Even with modest recent dips in some urban markets, average rent is still more than 16 per cent higher than it was before the pandemic. This is not just an affordability problem. It's a prosperity problem. A country where the middle class is maxed out, where essentials require debt, where upward mobility is on pause, is not a country building a future. It's a country managing decline.

Housing, once the surest pathway to middle-class status, has become a source of permanent anxiety. As we've seen, in Toronto and Vancouver the average home price is $1.2 million. In smaller cities like Halifax, Winnipeg, and Regina, the story is the same. Demand is rising, supply is stagnant, and affordability is a fantasy. In that context, the federal government's decision in 2023 to permit so many immigrants, international students, temporary foreign workers, and asylum seekers to enter the country, even as the economy created only two hundred thousand new homes, was sheer madness.

Yes, Canada needed the highest practical possible number of immigrants to fill labour shortages and ease the burden on younger workers paying for the needs of older citizens. But "highest practical possible" meant that infrastructure had to match intake. It didn't. The Trudeau government said we could grow quickly and inclusively. But we didn't build enough housing. We didn't invest in schools, in transit, in hospitals. Growth without infrastructure is not progress, it's pressure. And pressure creates cracks in the system. Those cracks can be found everywhere. Parents line up overnight for daycare spots. Newcomers live two families to a basement. In Indigenous communities, overcrowding and inadequate housing remain systemic. In emergency rooms, wait times can stretch into the next day. Immigrants are among the most affected. Despite high qualifications and a strong work ethic, many find themselves underemployed and overstretched. Unemployment among immigrant Canadians was 11 per cent in 2024, more than twice that of native-born Canadians, according to a report out of Toronto Metropolitan University.

For the first time in modern Canadian history, a new generation is coming of age poorer than the one that came before. And it's not just about income; it's about trajectory. The promise that if you worked hard things would get better has been replaced by a kind of ambient economic dread. The math doesn't add up. Buy a home? Start a family? Build a life in the community you grew up in? For millions, those are not goals. They're reminders of what they will never have. Canadians are beginning to suspect their leaders don't know what's happening, let alone how to fix it. They see a federal government that spent more than $500 billion during the pandemic—more, in real terms, than in all of the Second World War—while failing to deliver housing, control inflation, or maintain economic stability.

Various recent studies and surveys, including polls by Ipsos and Ekos, show that a majority of Canadians no longer trust the federal government to do what's right for them. Public trust in other institutions is also in decline. And as the legacy media continue to weaken, the public is losing trust in journalism, even as some areas of social media spew disinformation and discord. The political implications are dire. A generation raised on the postwar consensus is now questioning it.

They are skeptical of promises, cynical about politics, angry about housing, furious about affordability, and ready to punish anyone who tells them to be patient.

Added to all the stress from the pandemic and its aftermath is a new fear: Can we protect the Canada of the future? Can we even defend ourselves? How will we preserve our economy in a trade war with an ally that is rapidly turning into something resembling an adversary? Does Canada even make sense anymore as a nation? Donald Trump says the answer is no. Canada "makes no sense," he said. "Canada only works as a state."[1] The president has said the unthinkable. Is he right?

✻

Canada lives in a sort of strategic illusion. We tell ourselves we're sovereign. That we punch above our weight. That we matter. But the hard reality is that we have always been protected by geography and American goodwill. Canada did punch above its weight in the two world wars. And during the Korean War, when Louis St. Laurent was prime minister, defence spending accounted for more than 7 per cent of the country's GDP. Then it was 4 per cent under John Diefenbaker, 3 per cent under Lester Pearson, 2 per cent under Pierre Trudeau and Brian Mulroney, and 1 per cent under Jean Chrétien, Paul Martin, Stephen Harper, and Justin Trudeau.

Our military is underfunded, underequipped, and understaffed. We can't enforce our Arctic sovereignty. We can't meet our NATO commitments. As of June 2025, defence spending sat at just under 1.4 per cent of GDP. This is not just a military issue, it's a sovereignty issue. What is a nation if it cannot defend its borders—if it relies on others for the most basic guarantees of survival? For decades, now, we've avoided asking ourselves that question, content to shelter under the protective umbrella of the United States, confident that our nations' values were aligned, our economies integrated, and our fates intertwined. But what happens if all that is no longer true?

The world is entering a new era. Protectionism is on the rise; multilateral trade and security is on the wane. The liberal international order is being replaced by spheres of influence, nationalist industrial policy, and strategic decoupling. Whatever remained of the "special relationship" between Canada and the United States evaporated in March 2025, when Donald Trump announced sweeping tariffs on Canadian goods: Not after consultation. Not as part of a negotiation. Simply as an act of blunt force. The United States had decided to "monetize its hegemony," as Mark Carney said in June 2025.[2] The tariffs, which quickly became an on-again, off-again affair, were a show of dominance, designed to remind Canadians where we really stood in the continental pecking order. The effect was immediate. Economists predicted Canada would enter a recession or might already be in one. Thirty-three thousand manufacturing jobs in Ontario were lost in April 2025. Things will get worse.

It's not that Canada has nothing to offer. The world wants our food and fuel and minerals. But that could be a problem of its own. The Russians and the Chinese are openly racing to increase their presence in the Arctic. Could they be after *our* Arctic? And would the United States protect us, or join in the competition for the spoils? And at a time when we desperately need national unity and purpose, the cracks threaten to tear us apart: between regions, between generations, between Indigenous and settler peoples, between new arrivals and native-born. The worst possibility is that Trump is right: that Canada doesn't make sense anymore, that we have lost collective trust in our country and in each other, that we have lost identity, lost affordability, lost even sovereignty. As each crack appears and worsens, the whole structure feels unsteady; the very possibility of Canada becomes uncertain.

But you know that line from Leonard Cohen: "There is a crack, a crack in everything / That's how the light gets in." Every crack in Canada reveals potential for renewal. We don't have to manage decline; we can choose to rebuild. That choice must start with an honest accounting of the challenges we face. We hope that we have delivered that accounting in the previous chapters. But accountability is not despair. We can't improvise our way out of this—no more looking for ways to paper over the cracks. We need to make some hard choices, some difficult trade-offs. Canadians who came before us faced the challenges of their day and met them. Now it's our turn. It will take ambition and courage and sacrifice. But Canada is worth it.

ELEVEN

FIRST NATIONS, FIRST PRIORITY

On April 10, 2014, the Harper government introduced Bill C-33, the First Nations Control of First Nations Education Act. The act sought to establish regional or provincial First Nations school boards that would be controlled by First Nations, with a curriculum tailored to First Nations language and culture while meeting provincial education standards, and with additional funding available from Ottawa.

The new proposal was innovative and groundbreaking. It would almost certainly have raised the standards of education on reserve. Shawn Atleo, national chief of the Assembly of First Nations, endorsed the legislation, as did many chiefs across the country. But many other chiefs did not. Some saw the act as simply more federal intrusion into their affairs.

Others resisted the loss of local control over education by individual reserve governments. And some considered Western education simply another colonizing product, the latest variation on the destructive legacy of residential schools. Facing intense opposition, Atleo resigned and the government withdrew the bill. An entire generation of First Nations children lost the opportunity for a better education, which is the surest path out of the poverty, dependency, addiction, and violence that plague far too many reserves.

But from the distance of a decade, we can see that the act was doomed from the start. The Conservatives had poisoned relations with First Nations leaders by imposing strict reporting requirements on reserve governments. The legislation had been imposed from on high. The task force whose recommendations led to Bill C-33 was led by the president of the YMCA, who was not Indigenous. Given the generations of oppression and control by the federal government over First Nations, masquerading as education programs, no wonder so many chiefs rejected the bill outright.

We don't need to tell you what every one of us knows: the federal government's shirking of its responsibility toward Indigenous peoples—First Nations, non-status First Nations, Métis, and Inuit—is by far this country's greatest national disgrace. Its devastating present-day effects include: youth suicides six times higher than for the general population and eleven times higher among Inuit; incarceration rates ten times that of the general population; one in six Indigenous people living in housing needing major repair; high school graduation rates on reserves of less than 50 per cent, compared to more than 80 per cent for the general population; boil-water advisories that have stretched on for decades. No one in Canada should be living like this. And yet here we are.

But after decades of neglect and drift, there are spring shoots of hope. A new generation of Indigenous leaders is working to improve conditions on reserve. And Justin Trudeau's Liberal government was the first in this country's history to make Indigenous issues a top-tier priority. It may be the former prime minister's proudest legacy. The task ahead is to know what's gone wrong and what is starting to go right, and to build from there. The first and highest priority of all Canadian governments—of all Canadians—must be to ensure that Indigenous children born today lead far better lives than any who came before. We can and must achieve this goal. No excuses this time.

❦

For more than 150 years, Canadian governments sought to absorb and erase the culture and identity of Indigenous peoples. The chief weapon of erasure was the Indian Act. Passed in 1876, the act consolidated earlier colonial laws into a single framework that gave the federal government sweeping authority over the lives of Indigenous people. It defined who was and was not an "Indian." It created the reserve system. It governed Indian status, land use, band governance, education. It imposed elected band councils and gave Ottawa the power to overrule those councils. It restricted movement off reserves and outlawed ceremonies such as the potlatch and the sun dance. Until 1960, it denied First Nations people the right to vote in federal elections.

The Indian Act was a system of control. Its goal was clear: assimilation of the First Nations population within the general population. Indigenous peoples were expected to abandon their languages, beliefs, and institutions and eventually disappear into settler society. Those who earned university degrees, who became doctors or lawyers, who joined the military, or who married non-status individuals often lost their First Nations status. The law treated Indigenous identity as something to be shed.

The residential school system was not an aberration. It was a core instrument of control for more than a century. The first government-supported residential school, the Mohawk Institute, opened in 1831 near Brantford, Ontario, decades before Confederation. The system expanded after 1867 as part of a broader effort to assimilate Indigenous peoples. In 1879, the Davin Report, commissioned by the federal government, recommended adopting an American model of industrial boarding schools. That report laid the foundation for a national network of federally funded, church-run institutions.

In 1920, under Deputy Superintendent Duncan Campbell Scott, the government amended the Indian Act to make attendance at residential school compulsory for Indigenous children between the ages of seven and fifteen. The goal, as Scott put it, was to "get rid of the Indian problem," or as an American military officer first said, "to kill the Indian in the child." More than 130 schools operated across Canada. Children were forcibly removed from their families, forbidden to speak their languages, and punished for practising their cultures. Some never came home. The schools traumatized generations of First Nations children.

The Indian Act remains the legal framework through which Ottawa governs most First Nations communities today. It still determines who is and is not a "status Indian." It still defines the powers of band councils. It still restricts how reserve lands can be used or developed. It is a nineteenth-century law presiding over twenty-first-century lives. Canada remains the only Western democracy where a separate race-based legal regime still exists under federal law. It was created to manage a disappearing people. It continues to endure as a structure of control. This is not reconciliation. This is oppression.

In 1969, the Pierre Trudeau government attempted to eliminate the special status of First Nations completely, through a white paper (a policy statement) entitled *Statement of the Government of Canada on Indian Policy*. This galvanized First Nations leaders to cooperate in fighting the policy, and the Trudeau government eventually shelved the project. Ironically, the struggle to defeat it launched the First Nations protest movement, ultimately forcing Trudeau and the premiers to entrench Indigenous rights in the 1982 Canada Act.

Despite that guarantee, Canada drifted into postcolonial paternalism. There was this commitment and that policy and another round of consultations and reports. But the money, the services, and the real decisions stayed with Ottawa. The Truth and Reconciliation Commission, launched by the Harper government and concluded soon after Justin Trudeau became prime minister, produced a monumental record of residential school abuses. Its ninety-four Calls to Action offered a compelling moral case for reckoning with history. But most of the recommendations remain unfulfilled.

Canada also adopted the United Nations Declaration on the Rights of Indigenous Peoples and passed legislation to align federal law with it. But again, this changed little on the ground. The declaration affirmed ideals such as self-determination and consent but offered no roadmap for their implementation in a country where jurisdiction is already deeply contested. Instead, Canada gravitated toward a politics of recognition, including land acknowledgements at the beginning of public events. High on empathy; low on results.

Justin Trudeau resolved to change all this, although with mixed results and varied reactions from Indigenous peoples. He declared that Indigenous reconciliation and self-government would become a top-tier priority. Some of his government's achievements were indeed landmark. One was a $40 billion child settlement agreement. The chiefs initially rejected the agreement, but in 2025 both sides remained optimistic that they will reach final terms. The government implemented at least some of the recommendations of the Truth and Reconciliation Commission and reduced the number of reserves with unsafe drinking water.

Some of the prime minister's actions were more performative than effective: kneeling with a teddy bear in mourning for children who died at residential schools and ordering flags lowered for months; splitting the Department of Indigenous and Northern Affairs into two departments; taking Hector Langevin's name off the building housing the Prime Minister's Office. But at the least, Trudeau achieved what no other prime minister had even attempted: making Indigenous issues—

in words if not always in deeds—a major emphasis for the federal government. Miles of road lie ahead to close the gap between aspirations and outcomes for Indigenous peoples. To understand those challenges, we need some plain talk.

❧

With more than six hundred First Nations in Canada, and myriad different circumstances and needs, it is not surprising that leaders often disagree among themselves. The Coastal GasLink project in British Columbia had the support of elected band councils along its route. Hereditary Wet'suwet'en leaders opposed it, resulting in blockades, national paralysis, and a complete breakdown of clarity over who had authority. Some Indigenous communities supported the expansion of the Trans Mountain pipeline in Alberta and B.C.; others opposed it. The protests and court challenges delayed construction for years and added billions in costs. The Indian Act imposed elected councils; many communities still adhere to traditional leadership. There is no resolution mechanism for when structures collide. Projects stall, billions are lost, and no one is accountable.

Communities that prefer to be governed by traditional systems rather than elected councils should be supported. But those systems must meet basic standards of transparency, accountability, and democratic legitimacy. The same expectations that apply to any government in Canada must apply here, too. Self-government cannot mean exemption from responsibility. Similarly, First Nations leaders, federal and provincial governments, and ultimately the Supreme Court must find a way to reconcile conflicts within and between First Nations over resource development. A decade of delays as lawyers argue and costs soar serves no one. And when communities fail—through mismanagement, lack of capacity, or even corruption—we need to be honest about that too. Some of the current leadership is not meeting its responsibilities. Self-government must come with accountability.

Some working models have proven effective. The Cree of northern Quebec control education, policing, and health care with stable revenues from natural resource sharing. The Nisga'a in British Columbia run a treaty-based government with real autonomy. The Inuit govern Nunavut. Indigenous governments succeed when they combine rights with responsibilities and aspire to achieve measurable progress for their people. To accelerate progress the federal government must overcome its deeply entrenched paternalism, while First Nations governments must seek solutions rather than lean on grievances. Both sides need to accelerate treaty negotiations and streamline the duty to consult. Ottawa must ensure that Indigenous communities have the access to capital, infrastructure, and professional and technical expertise they need, and must stop clawing back revenues when communities show initiative.

Conservative leader Pierre Poilievre has embraced the idea of a tax transfer first proposed by the First Nations Tax Commission. In essence, companies extracting natural resources on ancestral lands would pay their corporate taxes, directly or indirectly, to relevant First Nations rather than to the federal government. The proposal would be, in essence, a tax-point transfer between Ottawa and First Nations governments. The proposal deserves active study.

Indigenous peoples are at the centre of Canada's resource future. Nothing major will be built without their involvement—from liquified natural gas in British Columbia, to critical minerals in Ontario and Quebec, to untapped energy and infrastructure corridors across the Arctic. Involvement must mean more than consent. It must mean ownership, employment, and long-term returns. This is especially true of the region that is turning into a fulcrum of Canada's future: the North.

❧

No region is more central to Canada than Arctic Canada. Its resource potential is enormous. And as the Arctic melts, new shipping lanes open. Countries are watching; some are already making moves on our sovereignty. The Canadian military presence is minimal, its logistical capacity weak. Canada's ability to project power in the North is fragile at best. Yet the people who live there, most of them Indigenous, are expected to stand guard. They are asked to hold the line for Canadian sovereignty while living in conditions that would be unacceptable anywhere else in the country. The nation's highest living costs, most extreme infrastructure gaps, and deepest service deficits are endured by Indigenous communities in the territories.

The Canadian Rangers are the tip of Canada's defence spear in the North. A part-time military force made up largely of Indigenous volunteers, they patrol the tundra and report suspicious activity while rescuing lost hunters and stranded researchers. They teach southern soldiers how to survive in a land that does not forgive mistakes. They do all this with basic gear, few supplies, and little recognition. This is Canada's Arctic strategy: give Indigenous volunteers a rifle, a red hoodie, and a thank-you. Then hope for the best. Meanwhile, Russia has built dozens of permanent bases across its Arctic zone, and China, calling itself a near-Arctic nation, is investing in shipping, mining, and research. The Americans fly overhead, too, while Canada lacks a single deepwater port in the Arctic.

And even as this country depends on Indigenous communities to assert our claim to sovereignty in the Arctic, they are not provided with basic infrastructure, proper housing, and reliable access to health care and education. This is not just poor policy. It is national delusion. Canada's inability to meet the sovereignty test of being able to secure its borders is nowhere more glaring than in the North. The Arctic must be treated as the country's most vital security concern. That means not only investing in equipment and bases, it means investing in housing, roads, airstrips, energy grids, communications, and basic services.

To get there, in the Arctic and across the country, Canada must stop treating Indigenous communities as dependent clients of the Crown. They are not wards; they are governments. They are partners. That means difficult conversations about governance, outcomes, and the hard work of building institutional capacity. It also means Ottawa must let go.

❧

Reconciliation in Canada has reached a crossroads. For decades, political leaders have offered symbolic gestures, apologies, and promises of change. Yet for many Indigenous people in Canada, daily life remains shaped by poverty, poor health, underperforming schools, unsafe housing, and limited economic opportunity. The rhetoric has run far ahead of the results. The 2021 census reported that about 1.8 million people identify as Indigenous, roughly 5 per cent of the population. The number of individuals with Registered or Treaty Indian status under the Indian Act is closer to 1.1 million. This is not an overwhelming population in a country as rich as Canada; it is a small population facing enormous and historic challenges. Which raises the hard question: Why can Canada not get this right?

The failure has been one of political will, not resources. Governments have reached for symbolism over substance, gestures over outcomes. If reconciliation is to matter, it must deliver measurable progress that improves lives and strengthens the country. Economic independence is the foundation. No community thrives without a secure economic base. For decades, policy entrenched dependency by centralizing decisions in Ottawa and strangling Indigenous entrepreneurship in bureaucracy. But we already know what works better.

In 1993, the federal and Yukon governments signed the Umbrella Final Agreement with the Council for Yukon First Nations. The framework sets out the rights and responsibilities of the eleven First Nations that have signed the agreement, promotes co-management of the territory's land and resources, and grants First Nations communities the right to establish self-government, giving them the power to create and enforce laws on their lands. Since it was signed, First Nations in Yukon have made great strides in narrowing the gap between the standards of living of the native and non-native populations. Gaps still remain, but the Yukon agreement is a template for what all levels of government can achieve.

Modern treaties in British Columbia and the North have replaced grievance politics with frameworks for ownership, development, and self-government. These communities show lower poverty, higher employment, and stronger local economies. Research confirms they experience less inequality and higher labour incomes than comparable non-treaty First Nations. Land claims are not just about history. They are about building the future. The First Nations Land Management Act, passed in 1999, has been a breakthrough, allowing communities to escape the Indian Act and take control of reserve lands. This has unleashed investment, jobs, and local control. Transactions that once dragged on for years now happen in months.

Resource partnerships also offer a path to long-term wealth. The Alberta Indigenous Opportunities Corporation backs Indigenous equity stakes in oil, gas, and renewables, lowering borrowing costs and creating ownership. It provides guarantees that allow communities to buy into major projects. LNG Canada in British Columbia has signed agreements with more than twenty First Nations, delivering jobs, training, and income. When Indigenous peoples are partners, development gets done.

Along with control over resources, education is the great equalizer. Canada has tolerated an unacceptable gap in the outcomes of Indigenous and non-Indigenous students. A serious reconciliation agenda puts education at the core, not with more bureaucracy but with local control and clear standards. The abandonment of the First Nations Education Act was a tragedy. But renewal is still possible, provided this time all levels of government work together cooperatively, based on three key principles. First, communities should band together into regional or provincial boards, to maximize efficiency; second, those boards should be administered by First Nations, with a curriculum tailored to First Nations languages and cultures; third, provincial governments, which are responsible for education, should work with the boards to ensure programs meet provincial standards.

The Mi'kmaw Kina'matnewey (Mi'kmaq Education Authority) in Nova Scotia shows how well this can work. After the Mi'kmaq took control of their schools in the late 1990s, graduation rates climbed from less than 30 per cent to more than 90 per cent, surpassing the provincial average. Local governance, culturally relevant curriculum, and high expectations transform lives.

Modern treaties and self-government agreements give communities the power to shape their destinies, along with the obligation to govern well and deliver accountable results. Accountability is the backbone of good government—the bedrock, for both sides, of reconciliation. This isn't theoretical; this is proven. In the United States, Native American nations exercising self-determination consistently outperform those under federal control. In British Columbia, the First Nations Health Authority and the First Nations Financial Management Board have demonstrated the effectiveness of Indigenous-led organizations at providing services under clear accountability rules.

After resource control and education comes the question of infrastructure. It is a national disgrace that some Indigenous communities still lack clean drinking water, reliable power, or safe housing. As of May 2025, most long-term drinking water advisories have been lifted, but about three dozen remain in place, and other communities are at risk. The challenge is not just installing a water-treatment plant; it involves training people in the community to operate the system, many of whom, once they acquire those skills, then leave the reserve for better-paying jobs. Infrastructure investments must have clear timelines, transparent budgets, and local partnerships that create jobs and build skills. Housing solutions should unleash private investment, reduce regulatory barriers, and expand Indigenous control. The Nunavut 3000 initiative, launched in 2023, aims to build three thousand housing units by 2030, with construction already underway.

Though Indigenous people in Canada make up about 5 per cent of the population, they account for roughly a third of federal inmates. Indigenous women account for half of federally incarcerated women. Community policing, Indigenous-led justice programs, and youth investments are part of the solution, along with the consistent application during sentencing of the Gladue framework, which recognizes the unique challenges facing Indigenous offenders and recommends that judges seek alternatives to prison or jail. But the most important solution to tackling Indigenous crime is to tackle the poverty, addiction, and lack of opportunity that cause it. As with so many other problems that Canada faces, the solution is education.

Above all, reconciliation must move past symbolism. Canadians are weary of gestures that substitute for action. Name changes, land acknowledgements, and symbolic flags are important and meaningful for many people, Indigenous and non-Indigenous alike, but they do not replace clean water, good schools, decent jobs, or safe homes. This is not an unsolvable challenge. With fewer than 1.1 million registered Status Indians, many of them in close-knit communities, Canada has the capacity to succeed at reconciliation. The key to that success is an agenda that delivers clear goals, real measurements, and public reporting. All people in Canada, whether Indigenous or settler, want governments to show that programs work, that tax dollars matter, and that reconciliation means opportunity, not optics.

Reconciliation is about building a country where Indigenous peoples are full partners in national success. The path forward is clear: expand economic self-determination, invest in education and infrastructure, settle land claims, strengthen self-governance, and focus relentlessly on outcomes. If we get this right, reconciliation will not be a project of national apology; it will be a story of national renewal and a stronger and more unified Canada. It's work we should have tackled a long time ago.

TWELVE

THE BIG FIX

We must face this simple truth: Canada is a resource-based economy pretending to be something else. We talk about innovation as though it were a religion while our pipelines sit on drawing boards and our electrical grids wheeze. We name-drop Silicon Valley North and the Technology Triangle as though oil, gas, timber, and food were things to be ashamed of. Yet the world is crying out for what we produce. And instead of treating our resource wealth as a strategic asset, we act as though it's a past we should outgrow.

Norway, for example, didn't make that mistake. It embraced its resource wealth, taxed it wisely, built a two-trillion-dollar sovereign wealth fund, and developed both world-class services and an extraordinary bond of trust between government and people. We could do the same. We should have done it already, but the conversation was hijacked by moralizing, magical thinking, and the fantasy of an economy that never matched who we are. What we need now is a modern version of John A. Macdonald's 1878 National Policy, not a nostalgia project. We don't need to chase yesterday's industrial dreams or copy someone else's tech scene. We need to double down on the country we actually are: suburban, increasingly Western, resource rich. That's not a weakness. That's our competitive edge.

Of course there is more to Canada's economy than oil and gas and wood and minerals. We manufacture. We offer a rich array of services: financial, advertising, commercial, digital. We build houses. We make cars and airplanes and clothing. We're a leader in artificial intelligence. But we should stop pretending that central planning can do what markets do better. Superclusters and innovation slogans haven't built prosperity. They've built waste, bureaucracy, and drift. We need to unlock private sector ingenuity, not suffocate it. The answer isn't another government program. It's a national energy corridor. It's streamlined infrastructure. It's open interprovincial trade and nationally recognized regulations and certifications. Let markets breathe. Let them build.

Governments need to get out of the way. Too often, bureaucrats have responded to economic challenges by managing the economy through tax incentives, regulations, investment vehicles, government loans, and grants. Tens of billions of dollars have been funnelled into electric-vehicle investment, much of which may have been wasted because of both American tariffs and lack of market demand. But it's not just the auto sector. In the main, government assistance does more harm than good, pushing investment to where some public servant or politician thinks it should go rather than letting the market direct itself. End the subsidies; eliminate every possible regulation, short of endangering public safety; make government small and helpful rather than large and obstructive. Markets settle arguments fast. When we embrace that fact, we win. When we fight it, we drift. And the drift is what is pulling this country apart.

And there's another problem. Canada is demographically fragile.

❈

The country's story begins in the cradle—or, more honestly, in the empty cradle, with a birth rate that has fallen below 1.3 children per woman, among the lowest in the world. Each generation will be smaller than the one before. Fewer babies today means fewer workers tomorrow, even as the ranks of retirees swell and lean harder on a shrinking workforce. This is not a distant crisis. Schools are already closing. The labour pool is evaporating. The balance between young and old is tipping, stretching pensions, hospitals, and services to the limit. As we wrote in *Empty Planet* (2019), Canada is not alone in its low-fertility challenge. Most developed and many developing countries have low fertility rates; some are in population decline. But Canada must deal with its own situation or face continued erosion of the population and a generational imbalance.

There are ways to ease the strain. One is through affordable childcare. Quebec showed the way in the 1990s, using subsidized daycare and family benefits to lift its birth rate from last place to near the top in Canada. Ottawa and the provinces are now rolling out a national childcare program, one of the Trudeau government's most important initiatives, though the emphasis should be on creating spaces, without regard to whether they are private or public sector. Childcare programs will not create a baby boom. But they will help families who want children to have them. France has stayed near the top of the European fertility pack with parental leave, tax breaks, and family allowances. Canadians are no different. Give them the right conditions and they will act.

But here is the harder truth. No government can legislate its way out of a birth-rate crisis. Having children is a deeply personal choice, shaped by culture, economics, and expectations. Policy can help, but it cannot do the job alone. That is why immigration has become Canada's main engine of growth. Without newcomers, the economy would stall. But immigration without integration is just a numbers game. Too many skilled immigrants arrive only to hit credential barriers or the wall of needing Canadian experience. A nurse practitioner ends up driving an Uber while the waiting list for health care providers grows. Thankfully, things are beginning to change. Ontario has scrapped the Canadian-experience rule for dozens of professions. Provinces are clearing credential bottlenecks for doctors, nurses, and trades. New immigration streams are designed to fill real gaps, not just meet quotas. Mentorship programs are linking newcomers with employers and breaking the old pattern of talent left on the sidelines.

Where people land also matters. More than half of newcomers settle in Toronto, Vancouver, and Montreal, straining housing, transit, and schools while smaller cities and rural towns empty out. Yet here, too, there is progress. The Atlantic Immigration Program has reversed years of decline on the East Coast, while Rural and Northern initiatives are doing the same across the Prairies and Ontario. These efforts succeed because people are matched with real jobs, real services, and real futures.

Beneath all this lies the skills gap. It is not just about how many people come to Canada, but about what they can do when they get here. A plan that ignores the mismatch between talent and opportunity is bound to fail. That is why credential reform, apprenticeships, and clear pathways into health care, construction, and technology matter. They are not add-ons. They are essentials.

All of this—market-based economic development, deregulation, immigration reform, improved childcare—is not a call for bigger government. It is a call for smaller and smarter government. Focus on what works. Cut red tape. Let businesses do what they do best. Let communities shape their own future. Make space for families and immigrants to build the lives they want without rules that block the way. We have the tools. We know the playbook. And the stakes are incredibly high. If we get things wrong, we risk permanent intergenerational warfare.

*

Canada is at risk of breaking its contract with younger workers, leaving many weighed down by debt and uncertain of their place in the country they are supposed to inherit. Immigration may help fill shortages, but younger people who were born here remain the engine of the workforce and our hope for the future. We need to offer them a better future than they have now.

For one thing, we need a surge in housing construction. But not one dictated by urban planners chasing fantasies of Amsterdam or Copenhagen, and not one driven by politicians who think housing is just a numbers game. The problem with Canadian housing is not just zoning requirements or permit delays or development charges—though they all need to be changed or reduced, even slashed. It is that we have stopped building the kinds of homes Canadians want and can afford. For most young people, according to survey after survey, the dream is not to live in a glass tower in a high-density neighbourhood, wielding their transit pass or riding their bike and relying on a local pocket park for greenspace. They want a house with a backyard and a place to put a barbecue. Canadians are not anti-urban. But they want space, privacy, and a future they can build around, not a lecture on how they should live.

The conversation about the housing crisis shows a clear mismatch between expert-driven supply and consumer-driven demand. If the experts win, consumers lose. For too long, the housing debate has been dominated by planners and politicians focused on densification of existing neighbourhoods. Too little gets built because existing homeowners fight each new proposal, and municipal councillors do what their voters tell them. But most Canadians prefer a single-family house in a car-commuting suburb. COVID and the rise of remote work only deepened this preference. Canadians want space for families, pets, and home offices, and they are willing to drive to get it.

The answer to the housing crisis is not just densifying downtowns or cranking out cheap government-assisted prefab units to pad the numbers. The answer is to expand the suburbs, build new communities, make sure the supply of family-sized, middle-class housing keeps pace with demand, with homes people actually want to live in, not just endure. The model is not just mid-rise additions to strip malls or office towers converted to lofts. It is new subdivisions with affordable homes, faster transportation connections, and smart regional planning that balances growth.

Yes, that means paving over farmland. Yes, that means urban sprawl. Most of us grew up in that sprawl, and younger people want to live there, too. Permitting sprawl is the surest way to lower overall housing costs. Once again, the best way to provide affordable housing is to give the market the space needed to build it. We should focus less on protecting greenbelts and agriculture and focus more on creating detached or connected suburban housing. We also need to invest in commuter rail, express buses, and highways that connect where people live to where they work. We need to recognize that remote work has rewritten the map and that growth can spread beyond downtowns.

And if existing homeowners have to pay for the infrastructure those new developments require—well, how do they think *their* neighbourhood got built? Property taxes on existing neighbourhoods help fund the development of future neighbourhoods. That's one way people can transfer some of the equity in their homes to people needing homes of their own.

None of this means ignoring urban intensification. But intensification needs to include cutting regulations and limiting the power of NIMBY. As well, suburbs need more variety, including duplexes, townhomes, and laneway homes. Municipal and provincial governments need to strip away zoning regulations that separate commercial from residential developments. If you want to build it—a housing development, an office building, even a factory, within limits—you can, without having to wait six years for a permit. We'll know the changes are working if we start to see corner stores once again popping up on residential streets.

This will upset homeowners who have watched property values soar and planners who imagine a Canada of downtown towers and no parking. But the alternative is a country where only the wealthy can afford the kind of home that past generations took for granted. The housing crisis is a self-inflicted wound, and we need to tear off the regulatory bandages so the market can heal.

Canadians want housing choice. That means downtown options, suburban developments, and rural builds. It means homes that reflect how people want to live, not just how planners or politicians think they should live. A serious housing strategy understands that success is measured not only in numbers but in the quality and livability of what we build. Only by building at scale, across all regions and housing types, can Canada rebuild the dream of homeownership and deliver the future young Canadians deserve.

Sprawl, baby, sprawl!

❧

Housing is only part of the deal. A country that promises opportunity must also deliver on the other pillars of middle-class life: education that leads to good jobs, a tax system that rewards hard work, and a generational contract that feels fair to those coming up behind.

We need to tackle student debt and rethink how we educate and train young people. Ottawa took a step forward by eliminating interest on federal student loans, but we can go further. Reduce or forgive loans for students entering critical sectors. Expand grants to reduce borrowing costs. Follow the lead of Germany and Switzerland, where apprenticeships and vocational training are respected paths to stable employment. Offer tax credits to businesses that train young workers. Make co-op programs, internships, and mentorships the norm, not the exception. That requires all levels of government to work together with businesses and labour to target need, establish workable programs, and respect certification, regardless of jurisdiction.

College and university administrations should be working with faculty to ensure that every program is designed for co-op assignments, internships, work experience, and mentorships. If the curriculum doesn't fit those programs, then should they really be teaching it? For postsecondary students, work experience should be the rule, not the exception. Also, there's nothing like a work semester to help pay for tuition.

Opportunity also depends on unleashing entrepreneurship. Canada has no shortage of young people with ideas. What we lack is a system that helps turn those ideas into businesses.

We need to cut red tape, lower start-up taxes, and make it easier to launch and grow. Denmark's digital-first government makes that country one of the easiest places in the world to start a business. Canada should aim just as high. We need to unlock intergenerational wealth through tax incentives that help older entrepreneurs pass on businesses, or that encourage relatives to invest in family start-ups, which could spark a wave of innovation. Britain's Start Up Loans program and Canada's Futurpreneur initiative show how a little capital and coaching can go a long way. We should help families transfer wealth when it matters.

Governments should offer tax breaks for parents helping their children with down payments and incentives for grandparents who want to support the education of their grandchildren or help them launch a business. Countries like Germany and Austria allow large lifetime transfers within families without heavy taxes. Japan offers tax breaks for living gifts. Canada should follow these and other examples. Introduce tax credits and exemptions that encourage families to share wealth when it has the greatest impact, not when it is too late to change lives. Build intergenerational mortgage tools that let parents and grandparents help the young without financial penalties. This is not just good economics. It is how we rebuild the generational contract and give young Canadians the future they deserve.

Canada's aging population is both a challenge and an opportunity. Healthy seniors should have ways to stay engaged through part-time work, consulting, or mentorship. Sweden ties retirement ages to life expectancy. Japan promotes second careers. Canada can link retirees with young entrepreneurs, create intergenerational teams, and offer tax breaks for senior mentors. Consider them investment transfers in knowledge, productivity, and social connection.

Generational fairness also means rethinking taxes and pensions. Young Canadians today pay steep taxes to fund programs that largely benefit older generations, with little expectation of receiving the same support when their turn comes. It is time to modernize the system. Means-testing Old Age Security for wealthier seniors could free up billions of dollars to expand childcare. And increasing the eligibility age for receiving public pensions would ease labour shortages, improve government finances, and help finance government services for older citizens. Stephen Harper's government took a first tentative step in that direction by increasing eligibility for Old Age Security from sixty-five to sixty-seven. Trudeau's government foolishly reversed the change. We need to go in the direction of keeping people working longer to pay the cost of services they need in later years.

The greatest burden of care for many people is the care they receive at the end of their lives. Some countries offer long-term care insurance, which allows people to invest, during their working years, in insurance that provides for their needs in their final years. Governments could encourage and contribute to such insurance. In the long run, it would lower costs for government while offering assurance to younger people that the resources they will someday need will be there for them.

As well, it's time we started talking seriously about mental health and the young. The challenges of finding a home to live in, securing a job, and starting a family in the uniquely difficult circumstances of our time can create enormous stress.

Australia's Headspace program shows the power of youth-focused hubs offering counselling, health care, and career advice without stigma or delay. Canada should follow that lead. Every major city and campus needs a youth mental health centre. Schools need more counsellors. Employers and communities can step up as well, supporting local programs and outreach.

We need to tailor these services to those most at risk, especially young men, who are often the least likely to seek help. Digital tools, sports programs, and targeted outreach can break through where traditional services fall short. Mental health care is essential to a productive workforce and a healthy society. Train more counsellors, bring mental health check-ups into schools, and enlist the private sector to help expand local programs. Prevention matters just as much as treatment. Financial literacy, life skills, and digital awareness programs in high school can reduce stress before it explodes into a crisis.

Above all, we must stop thinking of all these issues in isolation. They make up one big generational challenge: to give Canadians a fair shot at building lives of their own. They are the most important investments Canada can make. The country's future depends on whether its young can thrive. Give them affordable homes, a clear path from school to work, a system that rewards risk and innovation, and a society that treats their health as seriously as it treats economic growth. Do that, and Canada becomes a country of possibility. Fail, and we fracture along the deepest fault line of all: between young and old.

Now let's talk about the federation.

✳

The greatest threat to Canadian unity no longer comes from Quebec. It comes from the Wests, especially Alberta and Saskatchewan. Many in the Prairies see a federal government that does not understand their economy, does not reflect their values, does not respect their contribution, and no longer even bothers to pretend otherwise. The Prairies are not just angry. Under the wrong conditions, they could be finished. Finished with the national experiment. Finished pretending this is a country where their voice matters. Yes, there is anger in Western Canada among some. But among many others, there is something worse: detachment.

The Laurentian elite shrug it off. They call it a tantrum or a Western chip on the shoulder. They accuse Alberta premier Danielle Smith and Saskatchewan premier Scott Moe of undermining national unity in the face of Trump's tariff threats. They point to the deep pride Western Canadians still feel in Canada. They remind us that every time Western alienation has flared up, it has eventually faded. But they forget the damage it leaves behind.

Western Canada has always been part of Canada and never quite part of Canada. From the beginning, it was a place for businesses, many of them based in Toronto, to extract grain, timber, oil, and taxes without treating the region as a true partner of the Centre. Louis Riel saw it first. In 1869, he led the Métis resistance at Red River against Ottawa's push westward. In the end, after the Northwest Rebellion of Métis and First Nations, he was hanged as a traitor.

But he was the first to say the country was being built over his people, not with them.

The regional anger toward the East never vanished, including among those who arrived as settlers. It ran through the United Farmers, the Progressives, Social Credit, the Co-operative Commonwealth Federation. Every generation found a new banner for the same old grievance. We feed the country, we export to the rest of the world, but we are treated like a colony. The Reform Party turned that grievance into power. When Reform merged into the Canadian Alliance and then into the Conservative Party, Western voters finally had a genuine seat at the table. For a while, the Wests mattered.

But the pull of resentment never disappeared. It strengthens whenever Ottawa encroaches on resource development through regulations, taxes, or limits on pipelines. It feeds opposition to equalization. And after the 2025 election, the old frustration had a new edge. Pierre Poilievre's Conservatives had been ahead in the polls for two years. They seemed destined for power; the Wests would have true influence in Ottawa once again. But then along came Trump, tariffs, and threats of annexation. People in urban and suburban Central Canada voted for the flag and to protect their investments. The Wests were left out again: two Liberal seats in Alberta; one in Saskatchewan; a near shutout in B.C.'s Interior.

Former Reform leader Preston Manning warns that the Wests are on the brink of separation under Liberal leadership. "Large numbers of Westerners simply will not stand for another four years of Liberal government, no matter who leads it," he wrote in the *Globe and Mail* during the election campaign. "The support for Western secession is therefore growing, unabated."[1] Alberta is not just revisiting old dreams of independence. The conversation has shifted. There is even talk in some corners of a better deal with the United States. Not a hostile takeover but a clean exit. You may want to laugh that off. You should not. Prairie wildfires do not need much fuel to spread. Polls show that something approaching one third of Albertans are at least prepared to consider separation. When Quebec reached this level of alienation during the Quiet Revolution, Canada moved. We can do the same for the Wests, but it will take more than handshakes and empty promises.

We can't have a two-party system in which the Liberal Party alienates Western Canada and the Conservative Party alienates Quebec. Under such conditions, the country is bound to break apart. The solution is to strengthen national unity across the country. And one way to do that would be to partially dismantle the national capital. Nearly half of the federal public service is clustered around Parliament Hill, in Ottawa and Gatineau. That is not representation. That is isolation. It reinforces the message that Canada is run by the few, for the few, in one corner of the country.

We propose a major shift of government departments to Western Canada. Let's put Parks Canada in a park: Jasper or Banff would do nicely. If neither of those towns could sustain a full federal department, then move it to Edmonton. The department of natural resources should be headquartered in Calgary. The agriculture department could be situated in Winnipeg. And it would offer an entirely new and refreshing perspective if the Canada Council for the Arts and the rest of the heritage department were situated in Saskatoon.

The Atlantic region also deserves a full department. How about fisheries in Halifax? Northern and Arctic affairs could be centred in one of the territorial capitals. And how about situating the environment department in British Columbia's Kelowna? But the greatest emphasis should be on transporting as much of the federal government as possible to the Prairie provinces. The federal government should be *their* government, located in their cities, with many of the public servants from their region.

Ottawa cannot keep saying it values the West while most meaningful jobs sit within walking distance of the Peace Tower. When the Public Service Commission of Canada last updated its recruitment strategy, it talked about diversity. It talked about bilingualism. It never mentioned Western or regional representation. Why not? Relocating federal offices would do more than plant a flag. It would inject new, creative perspectives into the thinking of the federal government. It would bring jobs, ideas, and influence to regions that have too often been left waiting at the door. It would begin to break the old Ottawa reflex that sees the West as something to manage rather than something to trust.

Departments within all or mostly exclusive federal jurisdiction could remain headquartered in Ottawa and Gatineau: defence, foreign affairs, public safety, justice, finance. But every department that shares jurisdiction with the provinces, such as health and immigration, should be a candidate for dispersal. And we don't mean moving the public servants of a department out of Ottawa while the minister, deputy minister, and senior staff stay in the capital. The pandemic demonstrated the effectiveness of remote work. The minister and senior officials should be located where the department is located, dialling in for cabinet meetings, Question Period, and votes. When reporters asked Sean Fraser how he could spend more time with his children while serving as justice minister, he said he hoped to spend part of his time running the department from home. Let him be a lesson to all ministers as they work in departments that have been moved across the country, calling in to the Centre as needed. Dispersing departments might also weaken the stranglehold of the Prime Minister's Office and the Privy Council Office. It's hard to keep a tight leash on someone located thousands of kilometres away.

We would propose another consideration, especially for departments located in Western Canada. As we've written in the past, efforts to create a genuinely bilingual Canada have failed. The percentage of the population that can speak English and French has been stable at 18 per cent for decades. The bilingualism requirements of the federal public service disproportionately favour those living in the bilingual belt: cities close to the Quebec/Ontario or Quebec/New Brunswick border, where most bilingual Canadians are located. We would favour reducing or even eliminating bilingualism requirements for most public servants located in departments outside of Ottawa, especially for those departments located in Western Canada. This would ensure greater participation by Westerners in their own federal government, further broadening the diversity of views.

Critics will say that dispersing the federal government across the country will lead to further decentralization of political power. Yes! Much of the tension afflicting this country is the tendency of Central Canadians to wield federal power in the "national interest," which happily for them coincides with their priorities and preferences. Ottawa should dedicate itself to its core mandate of defence, foreign affairs, the border, justice, finance, and the like, and stay out of the jurisdictions of the provinces. Moving departments out of Ottawa to the rest of Canada would help ensure that the rest of Canada gets to have a say in what it considers the national interest, which might be a much more slender file than the elites in downtown Toronto, Ottawa, and Montreal would like to see.

The message is simple. If Canada wants to hold together, it needs to stop pulling apart. If the federal government wants to govern the whole country, it needs to live in the whole country. And if the West is expected to stay in, it deserves a seat at every table where decisions are made.

Next, Westerners need to see themselves in political decision making, regardless of which party wins the election. Cabinets with thin Western presence should stop handing out junior posts as window dressing while the real power stays in Ontario and Quebec. It should be a political expectation that every federal government hands a major economic portfolio to a Western MP. Even Pierre Trudeau, no friend to the West, understood this much. When he had no Western MPs, he pulled voices from the Senate to the cabinet table. We should not wait for another crisis to wake us up. Build Western power into the system now, not as charity but as recognition of its place at the heart of the country. Think of it as diversity, equity, and regional inclusion.

And there is something else we need to tackle, something that will chill the blood of everyone over fifty: it's time to reform the Constitution.

✳

Those who were around at the time still shudder when thinking about the agonies of the Meech Lake and Charlottetown accords. Efforts to accommodate Quebec's concerns in
exchange for that province's endorsement of the 1982 Canada
Act involved years of negotiations, acrimony, a failed referendum, and the near-death experience of the 1995 referendum
on Quebec sovereignty. In its wake—especially following the
Supreme Court reference on the terms of separation, and then
the passage of the Clarity Act—everyone agreed to leave constitutional reform at rest. It has stayed at rest for a quarter of
a century.

But the Senate remains unreformed. The Liberals fill it
with worthy progressives and well-connected Liberals; the
Conservatives say they would appoint card-carrying Conservatives were they in power. What matters more is that the
West is left underrepresented and Atlantic Canada overrepresented, with the Senate held in low regard by most Canadians.
There is still strong support in the West for the idea of an
elected Senate with greater Western representation from
Western provinces. Would Quebec ever agree to such a thing?
It might, in exchange for expanded powers over immigration
and culture. It might also be tempted by a proposal to for-
mally entrench the Council of the Federation, which is com-
posed of the premiers of the provinces and territories, into
the Constitution. The council could be given the power to
approve or veto any federal proposal that would interfere in
areas of provincial jurisdiction. And there could be regional
vetoes, including a veto for Quebec, within the council as well.

This would not produce gridlock. The premiers have worked together through the council now for more than two decades, with an impressive record on achieving consensus. Indeed, one proposal could be to abolish the Senate entirely, replacing it with the Council of the Federation. "Further weakening of the Centre!" cry the Laurentian elites. "Further decentralization!" We happily concur.

When it comes to Parliament, it is time to rethink how we represent Canadians. Proportional representation is not the answer. The idea has little support among Canadians, and for good reason. Its cheerleaders promise PR will end polarization and restore faith in politics, but someone forgot to tell Germany, Italy, and the Netherlands, where extremists thrive under PR systems. The problem in Canada is not how we elect politicians, but where they come from. In reopening the Constitution, we need to eliminate provisions that guarantee that smaller provinces are overrepresented in the House of Commons. Prince Edward Island has four seats in the House, which is just ridiculous for a province with a population of slightly under 180,000 souls. The electoral district of Labrador has a population of 26,655, according to the latest census. Mississauga–Streetsville, in the 905, has 130,345. That's just wrong. But P.E.I. and Newfoundland and Labrador might be convinced to surrender seats in the House in exchange for an equal voice in a more powerful Council of the Federation.

Could Canadians of this generation succeed where previous generations failed? Again, Donald Trump offers both a threat and an opportunity. All political leaders at all levels of government understand—or should understand—that this country is under existential threat, made worse by decades of laxity and internal squabbling. We fix things now, or we risk losing the country.

And speaking of fixing things, let's fix equalization. The policy was designed to smooth out differences in social services among provinces. But in the West, it has become a symbol of Ottawa taking and giving nothing back. When 62 per cent of Albertans voted in a plebiscite to strip equalization from the Constitution, they were sending a warning that Ottawa should not have ignored. Equalization needs reform. The formula is unnecessarily complex and screams out unfairness. At one point Newfoundland and Labrador were not qualified to receive equalization payments, while Ontario got some money.

The equalization system should be simplified. A deputy minister should be able to explain the formula with full clarity to a class of grade twelve students. Anything that would baffle those students should be jettisoned. (This, by the way, would serve as a good test of all government policies.) The formula should be rejigged to make the baseline for national standards and fiscal capacity that of the four largest provinces: Ontario, Quebec, British Columbia, and Alberta. Any provinces that lack the revenue capacity of the Big Four should receive equalization. What could be more fair? And to anyone who says that's not how equalization is supposed to work, well, that's how it should work now.

Under this formula, Quebec would go from being the biggest receiver of equalization to receiving no equalization at all, which could create a national unity crisis of its own. Any constitutional negotiation would need to protect the province's fiscal capacity. But preserving fiscal equilibrium between

Ottawa and Quebec should occur outside of the equalization formula, through some form of direct federal transfer. That transfer could be time limited, but subject to renegotiation. The long-term goal should be for the province to develop its economy to the point that it requires no federal support at all.

The reforms we've put on the table all push toward the same goal. Bring the West in. Share power. Let every part of Canada shape the country's future. Limit the federal power beyond its core responsibilities. Such a rebalancing could bring peace to the land for generations. And that peace would offer Canadians an opportunity to place pride over resentment, unity over division, and hope over fear of the future. And from that hope, we could renew not only our country's economic and political bonds, but even the stories we tell about ourselves.

❧

Our country is about more than economic and political bargains. It is a conversation among Canadians and between Canada and the world. We call that conversation culture. Historically, that conversation, that culture, has been muted outside Quebec, where a robust national dialogue ensures the province sustains its sense of self. Some aspects of English Canadian culture, on the other hand, have struggled to define what that culture might be. Instead, we binge on Hollywood, scroll through TikTok, and rage on X, living an American life vicariously.

The news isn't all gloomy. Much of Canada's cultural scene is robust. The country is rich in native-grown musical talent;

many Canadian authors are widely read at home and abroad. The theatre scene has matured considerably over the past fifty years, and the classical arts—opera, ballet, the symphony, chamber music—compare with the best in the world. But broadcasting—or more accurately, streaming—is troubled, and as we've seen, the news media are in serious difficulty.

English-language CBC, once the campfire around which Canadians gathered, is in grave decline. There was a time when it united the country with hockey, national news, and home-grown drama. Today, its share of English Canadian viewers is 3 per cent. That is not a typo. Three per cent. Everyone else is somewhere else: on Netflix, on YouTube, or tuning in to American networks. And the CBC's problem is not just about shrinking reach. It is about shrinking trust. Many Canadians outside the Laurentian bubble believe the network has been captured by a narrowly focused, urban, progressive elite, blind to rural, conservative, or faith-based perspectives. This country does not just need more content. It needs competing voices. A public broadcaster funded by all Canadians has a duty to reflect the whole country, not just the crowd invited to the better dinner parties in Toronto or Ottawa.

If we are serious about cultural renewal, we must start with two questions: Whose stories are we telling, and who gets to tell them? Culture needs friction. It needs risk. It needs arguments. If cultural funding becomes a closed circle of insiders rewarding people who think and talk like them, you do not get a national conversation. You get a well-produced monoculture.

Ireland's creative boom did not happen because the government told artists what to say. It happened because it backed its storytellers and then got out of the way. South Korea's pop music wave was not micromanaged from a ministry office. It was built on investment in training, studios, and global promotion. The Nordic countries pour money into culture but protect the product from political meddling. They fund art, not ideology. We should do the same. Funding models that support a wide range of creators across the political, regional, and cultural map will give us a culture that feels like Canada, not just the parts of it that control the scene today. The path to success in culture mirrors the path to success we've described for politics and the economy: decentralize and deregulate.

The Trudeau government sought, with all goodwill, to protect and advance Canadian culture in the digital age. But they went about it 180 degrees the wrong way. They offered a plethora of tax supports for media, accompanied by punitive regulations that sought to force streaming services to subsidize Canadian content and social media to subsidize journalism. The result is an expensive mess that has weakened rather than strengthened institutions. Let's do the opposite. Let's clear the field and trust Canadians to decide what they want to watch and hear.

The Trudeau government expanded the reach of the Canadian Radio-television and Telecommunications Commission into areas of streaming and media. Let's scrap all that. Instead, the federal government could set up a small bureau called Communications Canada, with no powers other than to sort out technical and licensing issues. Nothing else. And then let's do away with all the Canadian content regulations that the CRTC polices, and let viewers decide what they want to watch.

Let's reinvigorate the CBC by having it focus more on news and less on entertainment. Let's sweep away its over-burdened management structure and complex mandates, substituting a lean, mean, news-gathering machine. Let's replace all those upper-tier executives and governors with a national council that balances regions and viewpoints. Make sure there's an oil company executive on the council, sitting beside the head of an environmental NGO. Instead of what appears to be balance and fairness, let's encourage real clashes of opinion. Open the dialogue beyond the usual talking heads (including ours). Make the CBC professional, but also make it populist. Make it a place where conservatives, Westerners, rural folk feel at home. Make it truly national, not simply a Laurentian mirror. If five years from now people described the CBC as "messy," that would be the best possible news. A CBC that's messy is a CBC that's vital, that's alive.

The CBC need not deliver only the news. Canadians talk to each other through their sports teams and through cultural exchanges. That can also be part of its mandate. But whatever the broadcaster delivers, in whatever format, the suburban couple in the 905, the guys on the rigs in the oil sands, the Indigenous community in the North, the faculty club at the University of Calgary as well as the University of Toronto should be able to say: "That's my CBC." Not all of it, but enough of it to make them believe in it and watch it and pay taxes to support it.

And speaking of taxes, we should not be taking them from people to subsidize the new media. We should be doing the very opposite. Canada's legacy media are bleeding out.

Newspapers are closing. Local radio has gone quiet. Investigative teams are disappearing. Even some of our biggest national outlets fight to survive. Without a strong and independent media, Canada risks becoming invisible to itself. Worse, the hucksters and charlatans and crooks can get away with whatever they want to get away with. After that, the autocrats arrive.

Journalism is not just another business. It is the nervous system of democracy. Journalism simply must survive. But survival does not arrive through federal grants, grant-supporting councils, and extortionate efforts to force social media to prop up the legacy media. That only gets you what we've got: newspapers on life support, with just enough government largesse to pay the interest on the bonds held by hedge fund managers in New York. Let's sweep away all that and replace it with something much more likely to sustain robust journalism into the future.

This involves two steps. First, revoke all the Trudeau-era subsidies and regulations. Everything. Let them be gone. Then replace those subsidies with a generous tax credit to anyone who pays for a subscription to a news medium. It could be the *Calgary Herald* or the *Globe and Mail* or *Le Journal de Montréal* or the *Halifax Chronicle Herald*. It could be the *Tyee* or the *Narwhal* or the *Hub* or, yes, even *Rebel News*. Make it incredibly easy for media start-ups to launch and to reach out to potential subscribers. Let readers and viewers choose where to flow the funds needed to sustain journalism. Let the market decide.

The government could also help by making it easier to create non-profit journalism. This would be the second step.

Foundations, donors, and individual contributors could support non-profit journalism organizations that investigate anything that needs a shining light. Those organizations could send journalists into war zones, staff overseas bureaus, support rural news, or cover whatever most vitally needs to be covered, with no profit motive attached, with the results delivered through whatever medium makes the most sense and has the greatest reach. The United States is developing a robust suite of non-profit investigative organizations, including ProPublica, the Center for Investigative Reporting, and the Center for Public Integrity. Canada should encourage similar ventures here. This is not about punishing innovation. It is about encouraging consumers to sustain journalism by helping them pay the cost and letting them choose, and about fixing market failure through non-for-profit alternatives.

The goal of sustaining both Canadian culture and Canadian news media within that culture is the same: encouraging more voices, more independence, more choice. Journalism matters because, without it, we lose our democracy. A robust cultural landscape matters because, without it, we become strangers to each other. We need a living culture that captures the arguments, the joys, and the contradictions of real life in this country.

Finally, let's talk about how we defend ourselves.

❧

For decades, Canada coasted on geography and goodwill, convinced that peace came with the map. We believed we were safe because we shared one border with a friendly superpower while oceans protected us on the other three sides. We assumed no one would challenge us, no one would test us, no one would invade.

That world is gone.

Today, the global order is sharper, meaner, and less forgiving. Hard power is back. The nations that endure will not be the ones that talk the loudest about international law and collective security. They will be the ones that can stand on their own feet when things get rough. The situation for Canada is brutal. Our military is depleted, our borders are soft, our cyber defences are porous, and our industrial base is thin. We could get away with all that—spending money on social programs while neglecting defences—when America was a friendly giant. But the giant isn't so friendly anymore.

America is fractured, unpredictable, abusing its allies and flattering its adversaries. What if Canada were threatened and the U.S. refused to help? What if the U.S. *were* the threat? What if chaos spilling out of the United States seeped across our border? Right now, we could do little to respond to any of that. Canadians know this. In a June 2023 Ipsos poll, three quarters of respondents said they want to boost defence spending to protect Canadian territory. At around the same time, an Angus Reid poll had the same number rejecting the idea of leaving our security in American hands. The public is ready. Now the political class needs to catch up.

This is not about pleasing NATO or silencing Donald Trump at the next summit. It is about setting our own standards for our own security. A serious government does not measure its survival by NATO targets or by percentage points of GDP. It decides what it needs to do to protect its people and gets on with it. In Canada's case, that starts with rebuilding military readiness. The country's armed forces are aging, understaffed, and underprepared. We are short twelve thousand troops—16 per cent below target strength. Our CF-18 jets are older than their pilots. Our submarines are dry-dock regulars. Our Arctic patrol ships are only now arriving. In cyber, drones, and missile defence, we are years behind.

To see how far behind we have fallen, look abroad. Finland, with a population of five million, fields twenty-four thousand active soldiers and nearly three hundred thousand reservists. Israel, with nine million people, has a high-tech force backed by a massive reserve. South Korea and Singapore run national service programs that keep their ranks full. Canada, with forty-one million people, manages sixty-eight thousand active troops and twenty-seven thousand reservists. If a major crisis hit, we would scramble to mobilize one hundred thousand.

When it comes to gear, our procurement system is a slow-motion train wreck. Years of delay and bureaucratic inertia have left us waiting for equipment that should already be in the field. Even when money is allocated, it often goes unspent thanks to red tape and political games. Australia is showing how to break the cycle: it doubled its defence budget, cut bottlenecks, and rushed delivery of submarines and long-range missiles. We should take notes.

And personnel matters as much as hardware. We need to make military service a career worth choosing. That means competitive pay and benefits. No one who wears the uniform should struggle to pay rent. We should expand incentives, boost reserve recruitment, and create pathways for skilled immigrants to join the ranks. Canada should also follow Britain's lead and offer tax credits to employers who support part-time military service by their employees. A country that values its defenders does not just recruit them. It keeps them.

As we talked about in the previous chapters, the Arctic is no longer a frozen backwater. Russia has militarized its side of the pole with bases, radar, and the world's largest ice-breaker fleet. China is planting research stations with dual-use potential. Canada has fallen behind. That must end. New Arctic hubs in Iqaluit, Inuvik, and Yellowknife would help re-establish a year-round presence. NORAD modernization would bring over-the-horizon radar and satellite tracking. Arctic patrol ships and submarines would expand our reach. Canadians are watching. Eighty-three per cent of those in the 2023 Ipsos poll said they wanted the Northwest Passage monitored and 73 per cent wanted more military capacity in the North. The message is clear. Defend the Arctic or lose it.

But our security challenge does not stop in the North. The southern border, the world's longest undefended line, has bred a dangerous complacency. We wear that undefended border as a badge of pride, but peace is not a strategy. It is a stroke of luck, and our luck may have run out. Irregular migration across the U.S. border is rising again. Hundreds now cross between official ports each month, straining services and creating political tension. The drug trade is just as urgent. Fentanyl is killing thousands of Canadians every year and flows through our ports and crossings. We need chemical scanners at every major entry point, expanded surveillance, and coordinated task forces across governments and police forces.

The cyber front is equally urgent. China, Russia, Iran, and North Korea are already probing our systems—not just spying, but preparing to disrupt. Imagine a future conflict marked by blackouts, crashed networks, and financial chaos. That future is no longer science fiction. We need a national cyber shield. Israel's Cyber Dome intercepts cyber attacks, just as its Iron Dome intercepts rockets. Singapore has made cyber defence a civic responsibility. Estonia has a civilian cyber reserve on call. Canada, too, needs to harden critical infrastructure, build offensive cyber capacity, and expand digital literacy in classrooms. In the twenty-first century, cyber defence is civil defence.

And we must revive the defence industrial base. In the Second World War, Canada was an arsenal of democracy, turning out tanks, ships, and planes. Today, we are much more dependent on foreign suppliers. This vulnerability cannot stand. Other middle powers have shown the way. Many developed countries have smaller economies than ours but maintain thriving defence sectors. Canada has the bones to do the same. World-class firms in armoured vehicles, shipbuilding, aerospace, and satellites are already here. We need to scale them while supporting smaller companies and securing technology transfers in foreign deals. We need to accelerate critical mineral development, stockpile ammunition, and plan for surge capacity in a crisis. A country that cannot equip itself cannot defend itself.

In the end, defence is about people. We need a culture of resilience. Expand the reserves. Invest in cadets and rangers. Build a voluntary national service program. Procure fully and swiftly. Stockpile essentials. Secure our communications.

Harden our systems. Make every Canadian part of the national project, from cyber hygiene to community preparedness.

Bringing Canada's armed forces where they are to where they need to be will cost a great deal of money and involve sacrifice by all Canadians. Simply getting to the 2 per cent of GDP floor that all NATO members promised to meet a decade ago would cost an additional $20 billion a year. But NATO is now committed to raising that floor to an astonishing 5 per cent of GDP. For Canada, this would require many tens of billions of additional dollars in defence spending. But at the least, that kind of money would deliver a credible, essential military deterrent in the North. We are not advocating for specific increases in taxes, reduced services, or greater debt, though all may be required. We note only that other advanced democratic nations, from Australia to Estonia, have maintained a social safety net while spending a relatively high percentage of GDP on defence. If they can do it, so can we.

Does Mark Carney get all this? The early indications are that he does. In his June 9, 2025 announcement, the prime minister vowed to immediately increase defence spending to 2 per cent of GDP, and later that month agreed with other NATO leaders to move toward the 5 per cent target. He promised to increase pay, streamline procurement, and re-equip the three services. From acquiring over-the-horizon radar to bolstering cyber security to building defence industry capacity, the Carney government appears committed to reversing decades of decline.

But the shelves at National Defence are littered with defence reviews outlining bold visions that were never realized.

When we see budget commitments, procurement orders, and signed contracts, then we'll believe the Carney commitments are real. Not before.

A resilient country is not just one with jets and submarines. It is one where citizens know they have a stake in the survival of the place they call home. That is the real foundation of sovereignty. Sovereignty is not simply inherited. It has to be built, guarded, and earned. If we fail, we will not be treated gently in the new world disorder. If we succeed, we will emerge as a country that stands on guard rather than just singing about it. The choice is ours, but the clock is ticking.

❧

Canada faces a world that no longer plays by the old rules. As former foreign minister Mélanie Joly put it, the tectonic plates of the world order are shifting beneath our feet. That shift has exposed a hard truth Canadians must confront: we are not as influential as we once were. For too long, Canada's foreign policy has been shaped by mythology. We have clung to the image of the country that helped craft peace in Suez or rally global opinion on landmines. But influence is not an inheritance. It must be earned in a world being reshaped by rising new powers. Giants like China and India are asserting themselves. Regional players like Brazil and Indonesia demand a seat at the table. Even old friends are reassessing priorities.

When Justin Trudeau declared Canada was back on the world stage, he sparked hope that his government was committed to foreign policy renewal. But our failed UN Security

Council bids showed just how far our stock has fallen. Allies and adversaries alike have learned to tune out the platitudes. They want action. They want commitment. They want consistency. And when those are lacking, Canada gets ignored. AUKUS, which brought together the United States, the United Kingdom, and Australia in a pact to defend the Indo-Pacific, did not bother even to consult Canada—a blunt signal from close partners that we no longer figure in their plans. That should have been the moment Canada faced facts. Relevance is never owed; it is earned.

The way forward begins with discipline and realism. Canada cannot be everywhere and do everything. We need to focus on where we have something to offer and where the payoff matters for Canadians. This is not retreat; it is smart engagement. Australia offers another instructive example. When Beijing tried to punish it with trade boycotts, Canberra diversified its export markets, built new trade alliances, and stood firm. It worked—China eventually resumed dialogue. Canada can learn from this. Build resilience; deepen ties with like-minded partners such as Japan, South Korea, India, the EU, and the U.K.; and push back when others throw their weight around.

Once again, South Korea shows another path. Seoul transformed itself from an aid recipient into a G20 heavyweight by aggressively pursuing free trade, investing in technology, and exporting culture. This is the kind of focused ambition Canada should embrace. We have abundant natural resources, world-class universities, and expertise in sectors from energy to AI. But we rarely deploy them in a coordinated foreign policy strategy. Canada should be marketing its critical minerals to countries looking to break free of Chinese supply chains, packaging its clean energy and governance expertise as exportable assets, and striking trade deals in dynamic regions like India, Southeast Asia and the Pacific Island nations, and Africa. Trade diversification is no longer a slogan. It is survival. Today, roughly 75 per cent of Canadian exports go to the United States. The steel and aluminum tariffs imposed by the Trump administration showed how vulnerable that makes us.

Recent deals with the EU and the Comprehensive and Progressive Agreement for Trans-Pacific Partnership were steps in the right direction, but we need to go further. Smart trade policy is economic statecraft. It is time to use it. Canadians have seen what works. After the Canada–U.S. free trade agreement was signed in 1988, exports surged, fuelling prosperity. The test for any foreign policy initiative should be simple: Will it deliver economic opportunity or defence security for Canadians? If not, why are we doing it? Foreign policy is defence policy is trade policy.

We also need to be strategic about where we engage. The Arctic is an obvious priority. Canada should be seeking influence among polar nations while making sure any new economic activity among them works for us. The Indo-Pacific matters too. Half of global growth and much of the world's geopolitical tension come from this region. Canada's Indo-Pacific strategy needs to become more than a policy document. This means more diplomatic posts, more trade missions, and more targeted engagement with such countries as India, Vietnam, and the Philippines.

Multilateral settings offer another opportunity, but only if we focus. Canada sits at major tables—the G7 and G20,

NATO, La Francophonie, the Arctic Council—but too often we spread ourselves thin. Instead of vague commitments to a rules-based order, Canada should champion reforms that align with our national interest, such as cracking down on illicit finance, setting digital trade rules, and coordinating climate action tied to our natural-resource strengths. This approach does not require abandoning Canadian values. It means anchoring them in a tougher, more focused strategy. The United Kingdom, post-Brexit, scrambled to strike trade deals and to join the CPTPP, turning Global Britain from a slogan into a plan. Norway and other Nordics combine diplomatic skill with economic power.

Canada has a large, skilled population. We have natural resources the world wants. We have a diverse society that connects us to every region. What we lack is not potential, but will. Canada must stop drifting and start fighting unapologetically for its interests—thereby recovering the influence that comes from strength, clarity, and purpose. As history shows, when Canada has combined principled vision with resolve, it has mattered. We can matter again. But only if we are willing to do the hard work of earning our place in the world. The sooner we start, the sooner the world will listen when Canada speaks.

🍁

We are talking about big change. But none of what we propose is impossible. Some of it has been talked about for a long time around cabinet tables, in boardrooms, in classrooms. What was missing was a sense of urgency. Donald Trump's contention that Canada makes no sense and should disappear from the map as a nation may in hindsight be a blessing. Either he is right or he is wrong. Let's prove him wrong.

Canada has always been an improbable country—scattered across six time zones, with two official languages, a plethora of cultures, and no obvious reason for why it should all hold together, except for the determination of its people to make it work. Canada works because enough people believe in it. But that belief must be perpetually renewed. For too long we have coasted on the effort and sacrifice of those who came before us. If we want the country to endure, we must build again.

The thing to remember is that we have been here before, and come through. We created Confederation to prevent American annexation. When we were a population of only four million, we built by far the most difficult and ambitious transcontinental railway in North America. Canadians were admired by our allies and feared by our enemies in both world wars. We helped forge the alliances that have preserved peace among the great powers for more than eighty years. We built a great seaway, and ports and airports and highways and satellite networks. We participated in and helped conclude some of the world's most ambitious trade agreements. We fought off the threat of separation, just as we are going to fight it off again. We weathered the great financial crisis of 2008–09. We got through COVID better than most.

Now we must rebuild a Canada where young families can afford homes and futures, where Indigenous and non-Indigenous peoples share power and possibility, where each region speaks to the other in friendship, where we feel secure at home and are respected abroad. We have the tools, the resources, the people. What we need is the will to sacrifice what we must to create the best possible Canada. The choice, quite literally, is yours.

Are you prepared to vote for those politicians, and only those politicians, who advocate for what we've called for? Are you willing to sacrifice to help build our defences, and to do whatever it takes to make homes affordable for the young? Do you want to see your federal government transformed? Because what the next Canada looks like is up to you and your family and your neighbours and your community. The Canadians who came before us knew what they had to do, and did it. Now it's our turn.

Let's get to work.

ACKNOWLEDGEMENTS

FROM DARRELL BRICKER AND JOHN IBBITSON

Not for the first time, we gratefully thank Doug Pepper, publisher of Signal, and the amazing team at McClelland & Stewart/Penguin Random House Canada, who took on this project; Tara Tovell, who gave the manuscript her typically meticulous copyedit; and John Pearce, our agent, counsellor, and friend. What a run we've had! Thanks as well to Karen Alliston, for her impeccable proofreading of the book.

✤

FROM DARRELL BRICKER

This book was written in a matter of months, but its gestation has taken decades. Too many people to name have shaped what appears here. Most of you may not even realize how much you influenced my thinking, but I do. Thank you for taking the time to educate me, whether you intended to or not.

I want to acknowledge my colleagues at Ipsos, especially at Ipsos Public Affairs. I learn more from you every day than I can properly recognize. Thank you to Didier Truchot, Ben Page, Mike Colledge, Oliviero Marchese, Brad Griffin, Sean Simpson, and Clifford Young.

Others who have shaped my thinking about Canada include Allan Gregg, Angus Reid, Erin O'Toole, Ed Greenspon, John Wright, Sean Speer, Howard Anglin, Brooke Piggott, Rod Phillips, James Villeneuve, Troy Reeb, Ward Smith, Bill Tholl, Senator Pamela Wallin, Elizabeth Dowdeswell, Jeff Gaulin, Cal Bricker, and Joseph Bricker.

Finally, when I first began thinking about this book, the most significant influence was George Grant's *Lament for a Nation*. This year marks the sixtieth anniversary of Grant's great lament. The challenges he identified in 1965 as to whether Canadians can survive as a distinct people have only grown. But there is still time to choose our future. This country is worth fighting for. What happens next is up to us.

❦

FROM JOHN IBBITSON

From September 1999 until December 2024, when Darrell and I started work on *Breaking Point*, I served as a journalist at the *Globe and Mail*. That quarter century defined my life. To all the colleagues I served with, thank you from my heart for inviting me to join you on an amazing journey.

I still contribute to the *Globe*, the *Hub*, and the Fraser Institute, and as a senior fellow at the University of Toronto's Munk School of Global Affairs and Public Policy. To all the fine people at these organizations, thank you for inviting me to join you as part of the next journey.

Finally, to my family and friends, and to the people of Gravenhurst, Ontario, where I grew up, thank you for making that journey possible.

NOTES

PREFACE

1   Statement posted by Danielle Smith on X, 29 April 2025.
    https://x.com/ABDanielleSmith/status/1917211802665894381

2   Shaun Polczer, "Bloc Head Says There is 'No Future for Oil
    and Gas' in Quebec—and 'Probably Everywhere.'" *Western
    Standard*, 30 April 2025. https://x.com/therealmrbench/status
    /1917369187481313316

3   Andrew Cohen, "Canada's Return to the Politics of the Past,"
    Ottawa Citizen, 20 October 2015. https://ottawacitizen.com
    /opinion/columnists/canadas-return-to-the-politics-of-the-past

ONE: THE TRUDEAU EXPERIMENT

1   Stewart Lewis, "Pride in Canada Has Plummeted to 30-Year
    Low, According to Poll," *National Post*, 14 December 2024.
    https://nationalpost.com/news/canada/pride-in-canada-has
    -plummeted-to-a-30-year-low-according-to-poll

2 Rachel Gilmore, "'Fringe Minority' in Truck Convoy with 'Unacceptable Views' Don't Represent Canadians: Trudeau," *Global News*, 26 January 2022. https://globalnews.ca/news /8539610/trucker-convoy-covid-vaccine-mandates-ottawa

TWO: TOO MANY PEOPLE

1 William Lyon Mackenzie King, "Canada's Postwar Immigration Policy," *Alberta Online Encyclopedia*. http://wayback.archive-it.org/2217/20101208165211/ http://www.abheritage.ca/albertans/speeches/king_1.html

2 Marie-Josée Hogue, commissioner, *Public Inquiry into Foreign Interference in Federal Electoral Processes and Democratic Institutions, Final Report* (Ottawa: Government of Canada, 28 January 2025), 3–4. https://foreigninterferencecommission .ca/fileadmin/report_volume_1.pdf

3 John Ibbitson, "Jewish Canadians Living in Rising Fear as Violence and Vitriol Increase," *Globe and Mail*, 16 November 2023.

4 Justin Trudeau, "Why Canada Is Changing Its Immigration System," *YouTube*, December 2024. https://www.youtube.com /watch?v=vOB7-dbYuCc

5 "Canadian Public Opinion about Immigration and Refugees," Environics Institute for Social Research, 2024. https://www .environicsinstitute.org/docs/default-source/default-document -library/final-report94fae631-0284-4ba5-b06a-e0aeeab5daf3 .pdf?sfvrsn=9f47b717_1

6 Jordan B. Peterson, "Canada's Next Prime Minister: Pierre Poilievre," *YouTube*, January 2025. https://www.youtube.com /watch?v=Dck8eZCpglc

THREE: DUELLING ALIENATIONS

1   "First Ministers' Statement on Canada–United States Relationship" (Ottawa, Government of Canada, 15 January 2025). https://www.pm.gc.ca/en/news/statements/2025/01/15 /first-ministers-statement-on-the-canada-united-states -relationship

2   Statement posted by Danielle Smith on X, 15 January 2025. https://x.com/ABDanielleSmith/status/1879640059256914037? ref_src=twsrcper cent5Etfwper cent7Ctwcampper cent5 Etweetembedper cent7Ctwtermper cent5 E1879640059256914037per cent7Ctwgrper cent5 Ebf85b9640ab91ae2807bbb699ab3ca5e8db60d58per cent7 Ctwconper cent5Es1_&ref_url=httpsper cent3Aper cent2F per cent2Fwww.theglobeandmail.comper cent2Fpoliticsper cent2Farticle-alberta-refuses-to-sign-joint-statement-on -trump-tariffs-fromfirstper cent2F

3   "Statement: Premier Danielle Smith's Meeting with Prime Minister Mark Carney" (Edmonton: Government of Alberta, 20 March 2025). https://www.alberta.ca/release.cfm?xID= 930080FC1549A-0226-2967-AE8E7B92C734E9E7

4   Joe Bongiorno, "More Immigrants Are Staying in Quebec, Atlantic Canada Struggling with Retention, Report Finds," *Canadian Press*, 24 December 2024. https://www.cbc.ca/news /canada/montreal/immigration-retention-canada-1.7418547

5   Erika Morris, "What's in the Integration Bill Tabled by Quebec's Immigration Minister?" *CTV News*, 30 January 2025. https://www.ctvnews.ca/montreal/article/quebec -immigration-minister-tables-new-bill-aimed-at-better -integrating-newcomers

6   Lily Cheng, "Toronto City Councillors Jointly Sign Letter Opposing Federal Electoral Redistribution," 17 April 2023. https://www.lilycheng.ca/post/toronto-city-councillors-jointly-sign-letter-opposing-federal-electoral-distribution

FOUR: THE GENERATION GAP

1   Ipsos poll, 16 January 2025. https://www.ipsos.com/en-ca/43-percent-canadians-would-vote-be-american-if-citizenship-and-conversion-assets-usd-guaranteed

FIVE: OUT OF PRINT

1   Tatiana Siegel and Todd Spangler, "Joe Rogan and the Fifth Estate: How the Podcaster and a Group of Cable News Exiles Became More Powerful Than Traditional Media," *Variety*, 13 November 2024. https://variety.com/2024/tv/news/joe-rogan-megyn-kelly-podcasts-shaped-election-1236208937

SIX: CANADA ALONE

1   Lester B. Pearson, *Mike: The Memoirs of the Rt. Hon. Lester B. Pearson, Vol. 3* (Toronto: University of Toronto Press, 1975), 138.

2   J.L. Granatstein, "Fatal Distraction: Lester Pearson and the Unwarranted Primacy of Peacekeeping," *Policy Options*, May 2004. https://policyoptions.irpp.org/wp-content/uploads/sites/2/assets/po/governance-and-scandal/granatstein.pdf

3   Colin Robinson, "Canada's Defence Spending Isn't Just About Security," *Policy*, 3 September 2024. https://www.policymagazine.ca/canadas-defence-spending-isnt-just-about-security

4   Kim Richard Nossal, "How Good Was Harper for
      Defence?" *Dorchester Review*, 20 August 2019. https://
      www.dorchesterreview.ca/blogs/news/how-good-was
      -harper-for-defence?srsltid=AfmBOoqZx-JGjINjwEQ
      _UuBWlqnJVEr6uygvChdZiMdw_OWiFONRmS9o

5   Stephen Rodrick, "Justin Trudeau: The North Star," *Rolling
      Stone*, 26 June 2017. https://www.rollingstone.com/politics
      /politics-features/justin-trudeau-the-north-star-194313

6   "Trudeau Family's Attire Too Flashy Even for an Indian?"
      Outlook India, 21 February 2018. https://www.outlookindia
      .com/making-a-difference/trudeau-familys-attire-too-indian
      -even-for-an-indian-news-308603

7   Barkha Dutt, "Trudeau's Indian Trip Is a Total Disaster,
      and He Has Only Himself to Blame," *Washington Post*,
      22 February 2018. https://www.washingtonpost.com/news
      /global-opinions/wp/2018/02/22/trudeaus-india-trip-is
      -a-total-disaster-and-he-has-himself-to-blame

8   "Anger over Trudeau's China Remarks," *CBC News*,
      9 November 2013. https://www.cbc.ca/player/play/video
      /1.2421352

9   "Why Former Foreign Minister John Manley Thinks Canada
      Botched Huawei Affair," *CBC Radio One*, 18 December 2018.
      https://www.cbc.ca/radio/asithappens/as-it-happens-friday
      -edition-1.4946533/why-former-foreign-minister-john
      -manley-thinks-canada-botched-huawei-affair-1.4946539

10   Alec MacGillis, "How the Russian Invasion of Ukraine
      Upended Germany," ProPublica, 11 March 2022. https://
      www.propublica.org/article/how-the-russian-invasion-of
      -ukraine-upended-germany

SEVEN: THE ELECTION OF '25

1   Mia Rabson, "'Canada's Standing in the World Has Slipped'
    Under Trudeau, Marc Garneau Says in Autobiography,"
    CBC News, 5 July 2024. https://www.cbc.ca/news/politics
    /marc-garneau-trudeau-canada-reputation-suffering
    -1.7255120

2   Brian Platt, "'I Wish I Had Never Met You,' Wilson-Raybould
    Told Trudeau, She Reveals in Her New Book," *National Post*,
    14 September 2021. https://nationalpost.com/news/politics
    /i-did-not-trust-these-people-wilson-raybtoulds-new-book
    -reveals-battles-within-liberal-party

3   "Canadian Finance Minister's Resignation Letter," *Reuters*,
    16 December 2024. https://www.reuters.com/world/americas
    /full-text-canadian-finance-ministers-resignation-letter-pm
    -trudeau-2024-12-16

4   Larry Elliott, "What Can Canada Expect from Its Next PM?
    The Mark Carney I Knew," *Guardian*, 11 March 2025. https://
    www.theguardian.com/business/2025/mar/11/what-can
    -canada-expect-from-its-next-pm-the-mark-carney-i-knew

5   Catherine Lévesque, "'Look Inside Yourself': Carney Gets
    Snippy at Reporter When Pressed on Conflicts of Interest,"
    National Post, 17 March 2025. https://nationalpost.com/news
    /mark-carney-reporter-when-pressed-on-conflicts-of-interest

6   "Carney's Wordplay Is Not an Answer," *Globe and Mail*,
    15 April 2025. https://www.theglobeandmail.com/opinion
    /editorials/article-mark-carneys-wordplay-is-not-an-answer

7   Max Saltman, "Old US–Canada Relationship Is 'Over,'
    Warns Canadian Prime Minister," *CNN*, 28 March 2025.
    https://www.cnn.com/2025/03/27/americas/canada-trump
    -tariffs-response-latam-intl

8   Kate McKenna, "Tensions with N.S. Premier Simmered as
     Poilievre Made His Sole Stop in the Province," *CBC News*,
     24 April 2025. https://www.cbc.ca/news/politics/houston
     -poilievre-election-1.7518196
9   Spencer Van Dyck, "Doug Ford's Campaign Manager Accuses
     Poilievre Camp of 'Campaign Malpractice,'" *CTV News*,
     10 April 2025. https://www.ctvnews.ca/politics/article
     /doug-fords-campaign-manager-accuses-poilievre-camp
     -of-campaign-malpractice
10   Sarah Petz, "Ford Says 'Truth Hurts' When Asked About
     Criticism of Federal Conservative Campaign," *CBC News*,
     14 April 2025. https://www.cbc.ca/news/canada/toronto
     /ford-responds-teneycke-criticism-poilievre-campaign
     -1.7510103

EIGHT: LESSONS FROM '25: CONSERVATIVES

1   Elie Cantin-Nantel, "'It's All Garbage,' Poilievre Denounces
     Equity and Environmental Ideologies," *True North*, 1 August
     2023. https://tnc.news/2023/08/01/poilievre-dei-esg-garbage
2   Ian Bailey and Temur Durrani, "Poilievre Opposed to
     Alberta Sovereignty but Says He Understands the Province's
     Frustration," *Globe and Mail*, 13 May 2025. https://www
     .theglobeandmail.com/politics/article-poilievre-opposed
     -to-alberta-sovereignty-but-says-he-understands

TEN: A CRISIS OF CRISES

1   Allan Smith and Peter Nicholas, "Trump's Quest to Conquer
     Canada Is Confusing Everyone," *NBC News*, 14 March 2025.
     https://www.nbcnews.com/politics/donald-trump/trump
     -quest-conquer-canada-confusing-everyone-rcna195657

2   Campbell Clark, "Carney Sets Out Foreign Policy Shift as G7 Convenes Under the Shadow of Trump's Trade War," *Globe and Mail*, 14 June 2025. https://www.theglobeandmail .com/politics/opinion/article-carney-canada-foreign-policy -shift-g7-kananaskis-trump-trade-war

TWELVE: THE BIG FIX

1   Preston Manning, "Mark Carney Poses a Threat to National Unity," *Globe and Mail*, 3 April 2025. https:// www.theglobeandmail.com/opinion/article-mark-carney -is-a-threat-to-national-unity